I0073444

***

Tell me and I will forget.
Show me, and I may
not remember.
Involve me, and I will understand.

—Native American Saying—

***

***

We are in the process of creating what deserves to be called the idiot culture. Not an idiot sub-culture, which every society has bubbling beneath the surface and which can provide harmless fun; but the culture itself.
For the first time, the weird and the stupid and the coarse are becoming our cultural norm; even our cultural ideal.

—*Carl Bernstein*—

***

Bridging Cultural Barriers in

China, Japan Korea and Mexico

A Cultural Insight Business Guide

Boyé Lafayette De Mente

Phoenix Books/Publishers
ISBN: 0-914778-02-1

Other Books by the Author
[a partial listing]

[Books on Japan]
Japanese Etiquette & Ethics in Business
Japan's Business Code Words
The Japanese Have a Word for It!
Mistress-Keeping in Japan
Exotic Japan—The Sensual & Visual Pleasures
Discovering Cultural Japan
Business Guide to Japan
Japanese in Plain English
Survival Japanese
Instant Japanese
Japan Made Easy—All You Need to Know to
Enjoy Japan
Dining Guide to Japan
Shopping Guide to Japan
Etiquette Guide to Japan—Know the Rules that
Make the Difference
Japan's Cultural Code Words
KATA—The Key to Understanding & Dealing
with the Japanese
Speak Japanese Today—A Little Language
Goes a Long Way!
The Japanese Samurai Code—Classic Strategies
for Success
Japan Unmasked—The Character & Culture
of the Japanese
Elements of Japanese Design—Understanding &
Using Japan's Classic *Wabi-Sabi-Shibui* Concepts
Sex and the Japanese—The Sensual Side of Japan
Samurai Strategies—42 Secret Martial Arts from
Musashi's "Book of Five Rings"

[Books on China]
The Chinese Mind—Understanding Traditional Chinese
Beliefs and Their Influence on Contemporary Culture
Chinese Etiquette & Ethics in Business
China's Cultural Code Words [Key Chinese Terms that
Reveal the Culture and Mindset of the Chinese]
Chinese in Plain English
Survival Chinese
Instant Chinese
Etiquette Guide to China—Know the Rules that
Make the Difference

[Books on Korea]
Korean Business Etiquette
Korean in Plain English
Korea's Business & Cultural Code Words
Etiquette Guide to Korea— Know the Rules that
Make the Difference
Instant Korean
Survival Korean

[Books on Mexico]
Why Mexicans Think & Behave the Way They Do—The
Cultural
Factors that Created the Character & Personality
of the Mexican People
Mexican Cultural Code Words [hard-cover]
There's a Word for It in Mexico [paperback]

[Other Titles]
Which Side of Your Brain Am I Talking To? – The
Advantages of Using Both Sides of Your Brain
How to Measure the Sexuality of Men & Women by
Their Facial Features (ebook)

Samurai Principles & Practices that will Help Preteens &
Teens in School, Sports, Social Activities
& Choosing Careers
Romantic Hawaii—Sun, Sand, Surf & Sex
Romantic Mexico—The Image & the Realities
Women of the Orient
The Sensual Side of the Orient—A Traveler's
Arm-Chair Guide, (e-book)
Asian Face Reading—Unlock the Secrets Hidden
in the Human Face
Once a Fool—From Japan to Alaska by
Amphibious Jeep

*Various titles published in Chinese, Czech, French,
German,
Hebrew, Italian, Indonesian, Japanese, Polish,
Portuguese, Russian & Spanish.*

PREFACE

The Pitfalls of Logic
in Dealing with Foreign Cultures

INTRODUCTION

"Key Words" Provide Short-Cut
to Understanding Foreign Cultures

CHINA
[1]
The Cultural Influence
of the Chinese Language
[2]
Understanding the Yin-Yang Principle
in Chinese Culture
[3]
Dealing With Three Kinds of Logic
in China
[4]
The Imperative of
"Sincerity plus Understanding" in China

JAPAN

[3]
The Japanese Language as a
Cultural Obstacle
[4]
The "Indulgent Love" Factor
in Japanese Relationships and Management
[5]
Creating and Sustaining
Important Relationships in Japan
[6]
Nemawashi [Nay-mah-wah-she]
One of the Secrets of Doing Business in Japan
[7]
Japan's Do-or-Die Cultural Syndrome!
[8]
Japan's Built-in Cultural Obsession
with Quality
[9]
The Importance of Dealing
with Japan's Dynamic Diligence Factor!
[10]
The Japanese Secret
of Mastering Anything!
[11]
How the Japanese Build Success
into their Products
[12]
How the Japanese
Tap Into Cosmic Creativity!

The Pitfalls of Logic
In Dealing with Foreign
Cultures

WESTERNERS, particularly Americans, endeavoring to negotiate business and political deals in Asia often face a barrier that is so subtle, so unexpected, they do not know how to deal with it. They typically spend an inordinate amount of time and energy in an effort to explain their goals and methods and get their foreign counterparts to understand and accept them, with little or no success.

On these occasions the automatic response of most Americans and other Westerners is to assume that it is a simple language problem—that their counterparts don't really understand the points they are making, and begin repeating themselves.

In these repeated efforts some talk a little louder. Others assume it is a language problem and attempt to break their presentations down into simpler terms. Many end up watering down their original objectives in order to get a deal.

The degree of the impasse and the level of frustration that develops in typical Americans and other Westerners varies with how internationalized or "Westernized" their foreign counterparts have become, but there is almost always resistance on some level by the Asian side that Westerners cannot fathom or readily accept.

This situation arises from the fact that Western businesspeople and diplomats have been culturally conditioned to base their thinking and behavior on facts as they perceive them and on the logical progression of these facts. Their presentations and negotiations are normally reflections of this deeply embedded mindset.

In Asian, Arabic, Hispanic, Islamic and some other societies it is generally not hard facts and unadulterated Anglo-Western style logic that carries the day. It is human relations and feelings, past relationships, racial differences and religious beliefs—all of which to the Anglo mindset can be irrational and shortsighted.

For the most part, Asians, Arabs, Hispanics, Moslems and others are motivated by a variety of cultural obligations that must be met before they can whole-heartedly accept and pursue projects presented to them. In fact, it is not too much of a stretch to say that many people around the world, particularly those outside the Anglo-Western sphere of influence, are culturally allergic to pure logic.

In other words, *luoji* (luu-oh-jee) is Chinese logic; *ronri* (rone-ree) is Japanese logic; *nolli* (nohl-lee) is Korean logic, *lógica* is Hispanic logic, and so on, and they are defined by the cultures in which they developed—not the Anglo-Western definition of the term.

People in Mexico and the three Asian countries named above who *do accept* American and other propositions and/or responsibilities that they do not like generally do so by rationalizing that it is better to have a bad bargain [from their viewpoint] than no bargain.

And certainly in most Asian countries there is the unspoken intent to take advantage of Western relationships and technology by gradually subverting them to conform to their own views and needs.

It is therefore imperative that Americans and other Westerners who are driven by their own facts and logic to make a serious effort to discover how and why their potential foreign partners think and behave the way they do.

This entails an in-depth knowledge of the history of the people in question, including their racial ancestry, their underlying philosophical and religious beliefs, their political systems, their economic systems, their relationships with other people, and their languages.

But it goes without saying that the education system in the United States in particular either downplays or ignores altogether the importance of this level of knowledge about other people, and until this shortcoming is recognized and overcome we will continue to have political and economic conflicts in our foreign relations.

The cross-cultural myopia that is especially characteristic of mainstream Americans, including those on the highest levels of leadership, has obviously contributed to virtually all of the international problems we have had in the past, and is even more of a threat in today's world.

Remarkably, the election of Barak Obama as president of the United States in 2008 was a cultural breakthrough for the American people—a breakthrough that hopefully will help slow the degeneration of American culture, speed up the growth of commonsense in the American mindset, and result in the foreign reaction to American overtures and efforts becoming more objective and rational.

Boyé Lafayette De Mente

***

Our attitude toward our own culture has recently been characterized by two qualities, braggadocio and petulance. Braggadocio—empty boasting of American power, American virtue, American knowhow—has dominated our foreign relations now for some decades. Here at home—within the family, so to speak—our attitude to our culture expresses a superficially different spirit, the spirit of petulance.
Never before, perhaps, has a culture been so fragmented into groups, each full of its own virtue, each annoyed and irritated at the others.
—*Daniel J. Boorstin*—

***

INTRODUCTION

"Key Words" Provide Short-Cut To Understanding Cultures

DEFINING PEOPLE by their race while virtually ignoring their ethnicity has always been both dumb and dangerous, but now, finally, the importance of understanding cultures is rapidly becoming a new mantra for business leaders as well as diplomats and some politicians.

For most people, however, understanding the cultures of others is a process that requires long periods of living in and personally experiencing their attitudes and behavior—often preceded or combined with extensive studies of research by anthropologists and sociologists.

But there is an easier and faster way of getting into and understanding the mindset of people. While working in Asia and Mexico as a trade journalist in the 1950s and 60s I learned that the attitudes and behavior of the Chinese, Japanese, Koreans and Mexicans were summed up in a few hundred key words in their languages—words that explained *why* they thought and behaved the way they did.

I first became aware of the role that key words play in the mindset and behavior of the Japanese in my attempts to explain their way of thinking and doing things to American importers who began flocking to Japan in the early 1950s.

I made use of this key-word approach in my first book, *Japanese Etiquette & Ethics in Business*, published in 1959 [and still in print at McGraw-Hill], introducing the international business community to such terms as *wa* (harmony), *nemawashi* (behind the scenes consensus-building), *tatemae* (a facade or front in conversations and negotiations) and *honne* (the real intentions, the real meaning of the speaker).

The more I got into the Japanese, Korean, Chinese and Mexican way of thinking and doing things the more obvious it became that they were culturally programmed and controlled by key words in their languages, and that these words provided a short-cut to understanding them.

Further experiences in other countries confirmed that the beliefs and behavior of people in all societies—especially older societies—are primarily programmed by their native language and that learning the meaning and everyday use of key words in the language reveals in precise detail *what* they have been conditioned to believe and *why* they behave the way they do.

This led me in the 1980s and 90s to write a series of "cultural code word" books on China, Japan, Korea and Mexico in which I identified and defined—in all of their cultural nuances—several hundred key words in the languages concerned.

The fact that you must be intimately familiar with key terms in the native language of a people in order to fully understand their thinking and behavior is of incredible importance, but it is not yet common knowledge even among scholars and educators, much less diplomats, politicians and the international business community.

This failure to perceive and understand the role of languages in human behavior is one of the primary reasons why the world is continuously roiled by misunderstandings, friction and violence. We do not communicate fully and effectively across the cultural barriers built into languages.

Now there is another language factor that must be taken into consideration in communicating within and across cultures, and that is the growing incidence of the creation of new words and the application of new meanings and uses to existing terms—a phenomenon that is often disruptive and dangerous since it creates addition barriers to understanding.

In all advanced countries, the U.S. and Japan in particular, these new terms have created cultural gaps between the generations resulting in tension and friction that is revolutionary in nature.

Languages, Not Things, Preserve and Transmit Culture!

Most people still today mistakenly regard the arts and crafts of individual societies as their "culture." Arts and crafts reflect culture but they do not create it and they do not transmit it. You can view and collect Chinese or Eskimo artifacts all your life and you will not become fully conversant with the cultures that created them.

Despite the fact that in today's world languages are evolving they remain—at any particular time—the repository as well as the transmitter of cultures. They contain the essence, the tone, the flavor and the spirit of cultures, and serve as doorways to understanding them—and this critical role of language in the attitudes and behavior of people provides irrefutable evidence that to become American in the fullest sense one must learn American English as it is spoken by old as well as new generations.

It is fairly simple to interpret or translate technical subjects from one language into another, but translating cultural attitudes and values into another language ranges from difficult to impossible. The translations may be perfectly correct as far as the words are concerned, but they seldom if ever include all of the cultural nuances that are bound up in the words and are the essence of the original language.

Among the advanced nations, we Americans are the least sensitive to the cultural differences that separate people, and therefore continue to make mistakes when interacting with other cultures.

This problem will continue until the study of other cultures becomes a fundamental part of the education we all receive in our youth. In fact, I propose that the role of languages in the values and behavior of people be made a mandatory ongoing course in all schools.

Translation Devices Reduce But Do Not Prevent Misunderstandings

Throughout history languages have separated human beings into exclusive groups, making communication difficult or impossible, exacerbating their cultural differences and contributing to wars and other kinds of violence.

Again, the primary reason for this linguistic plague is the fact that languages are the reservoir, the transmitter, and the controller of cultures, so people who speak different languages have problems because they think and behave in different ways.

But technology is on the verge of eliminating many of the linguistic barriers that separate human beings—and much sooner than one might think.

Most of the world is familiar with the "universal language" devices used by the fictional Capt. James T. Kirk and the intrepid crew of *Star Trek* to communicate with the various life-forms they encountered during their travels around the galaxies.

Now, reality is rapidly catching up with science fiction. In 2008 Japan's *Council for Science and Technology Policy* challenged the country's automated speech translation researchers to improve the technology to the point that automated translators would be a reality for Japanese who wanted to communicate with English and Mandarin speakers.

Before the end of 2008 prototypes of these translators were field-tested in China, and the report was that they worked perfectly as long as the conversations were simple. The CSTP then announced its goal of having universal translators on the market for all of the world's major languages.

Obviously, this revolutionary advance in the growing ability of human beings to communicate with each other across language barriers will continue to increase the volume of conversations in business, diplomatic and personal encounters, and contribute to better understanding and more cooperation.

In fact, the impact this ability will have on the diverse people of the world is so profound and broad that over a period of a few generations it will surely change the nature of human cultures.

But no matter how good universal translators become they will not mean the end of cross-cultural misunderstandings and the conflicts that arise from them; nor will they eliminate the need for bilingual and multilingual people, experts on the various cultures, and translators skilled in explaining their own cultures.

Again, every language contains words that are impregnated with cultural meanings and nuances that are responsible for programming the minds and controlling the behavior of the people who use that language...words that have meanings and uses that are different from their stark translations into other languages.

This means that such words must be explained in detail to make the communication complete. As helpful as universal translators are and will be in the future their use is not going to eliminate the need for people who know both the languages and the cultures of their foreign counterparts, partners and competitors.

There is simply too much subtlety, too much individual variation in human feelings and needs, for a technical device to deal effectively with all of the situations human beings get involved in.

To fully explain the cultural content and role of the Chinese term *guanxi* (gwahn-she), or "connections," for example, requires several hundred words. To fully explain the Japanese term *kaizen* (kigh-zen), or "continuous improvement," requires as many as a thousand words or more (there is a whole book on the subject). You cannot understand Mexican attitudes and behavior without known the full cultural meaning and use of the word *simpatico* (seem-PAH-tee-co).

There are also numerous commonly used expressions in languages that mean something quite different from the content of the words themselves—and unless you know the real meanings of these phrases you can be totally mislead.

Such expressions are especially common in Japanese, Chinese, Korean—and English. One of the most misleading of the Japanese expressions is *Zensho shimasu*

[Zen-show she-mahss], which is usually translated as "I will do my best" or "I will take care of it."

The typical Westerner takes this as meaning that something will be done. In actuality, it is a culturally acceptable way of saying it can't or won't be done—a point that is clearly understood by all Japanese.

I have used the "key word" approach to identifying some of the most common cultural barriers between Chinese, Japanese, Koreans, Mexicans and the rest of the world that, hopefully, will help Americans and others understand and deal more effectively with these cultural differences.

***

Letting a hundred flowers blossom and a hundred schools of thought contend is the policy for promoting the progress of the arts and the sciences and a flourishing culture in our land.

—Mao Zedong—
[1893-1976]

***

CHINA

[1]
The Extraordinary Influence
Of China's Language and
Writing Systems

THERE ARE A dozen or more fundamental elements of Chinese culture that make it different from Western cultures, but just one of these elements provides deep insight into the differences in their mindset and behavior.

This one element is the use of *Han zi* (Hahn-jee), literally meaning "Chinese characters," which the Chinese and the Japanese and Koreans] have traditionally used to transcribe their languages. [The better known Japanese version of this designation is *Kahn ji* [Kahn jee]...and generally both *Han zi* and *Kan ji* are written as one word when transcribed into Roman letters.]

Hanzi originated in China between five and six thousand years ago and eventually numbered around 250,000 characters—a number that was gradually pared down over the millennia, and is now around 5,000 for scholars and from 4,000 to 2,000 for ordinary people.

All *Hanzi* are based on the stylization of concepts, objects and other things from real life. In other words, they are "pictures" of things that have inherent meanings—not just substitutes for sounds as in the Roman alphabet.

Furthermore, unlike the simple Roman alphabet, Chinese characters consist of one to as many as thirty or more individual "strokes" that must "fit" together, and by long tradition must be drawn in a precise order.

The Chinese *Hanzi* system of writing was imposed on Koreans more than two thousand years ago and was adopted by the Japanese between the 6th and 7th centuries A.D.

By 1,000 B.C. one of the key measurements of the cultural achievements of educated Chinese was how many of the characters they could read and write. As time went by how artistically they could render the characters as *shufa* (shuu-fah) or calligraphy became more and more important.

This same phenomenon occurred in both Korea and Japan, with the greatest calligraphy masters becoming historical icons who are still remembered and celebrated today. By the 1700s even Japan's notorious samurai warriors took as much pride in their ability to draw *Kanji* as calligraphy, known as *shodō* [show-dohh] in Japanese, as they did in their skill in drawing and using their deadly swords.

The point of this is that learning how to read and draw large numbers of the intricate *Hanzi* has had a profound influence on the mindset and manual skills of the Chinese, Japanese and Korean since ancient times.

Still today from their earliest years in kindergarten and elementary schools, learning how to draw some two thousand ideograms forces them to focus with laser-like intensity on the characters and to develop eye-and-hand coordination that influences the rest of their lives.

Learning to read and draw the ideograms requires not only intense concentration but perseverance, acute concern with the finest details, and an appreciation for form, harmony and function—all characteristics that are associated with the mindset of adult Chinese, Japanese and Koreans in all of their affairs, from meticulous planning in business to scientific research.

Westerners, on the other hand, are expected to learn how to pronounce the sounds and to draw only twenty-six letters that by themselves have no meaning. This alone accounts for much of the contrast between the academic prowess of Westerners and their Chinese, Japanese and Korean counterparts.

Another important contrast between Westerners and Hanzi-influenced Asians is that popular Western culture—American culture in particular—now de-emphasizes long periods of concentration and meticulous effort in favor of speed and superficiality in everything, from education to manufacturing and entertainment.

This is a cultural weakness that threatens the future of the United States and other Western countries, and is a barrier that cannot be eliminated in a short time because it has become an inseparable part of the mindset and lifestyle of most Westerners.

Until well into the 20th century educated Europeans and Americans at least learned how to write the Roman alphabet clearly and often beautifully. Now, even mediocre handwriting appears to be on its way out.

I am not proposing that Americans and other Westerners learn how to transcribe their languages in Chinese ideograms, but unless we act to upgrade the level of our culture we will continue to be at a disadvantage in dealing with people programmed by their intense exposure to *Hanzi*.

There are, of course, links between the languages of the West that evolved from or were influenced by the Latin language, spread across much of Western Europe by the Roman Empire.

These Latin links have significantly influenced the cultures they merged with. But even Latin-linked cultures that are as close as American and British have language-based differences that are profound, and if not taken into consideration can—and do—lead to misunderstandings and gaps in cross-cultural communication.

It has been proven time and again that a gap in communication of less than one percent can eventually lead to serious problems if not recognized and remedied in a timely manner.

To understand and appreciate the role and importance of Hanzi in Chinese culture one would have to imagine that all of the European societies that came under the influence of the Roman Empire adopted the written form of Latin to transcribe their languages but retained much of their own system of pronunciation.

That is exactly what happened among China's fifty-three ethic groups that originally had and still have the own languages. Twenty-three of these minority groups had their own writing systems.

Over centuries, these diverse groups of people gradually adopted Hanzi to write their languages. They kept the meanings of the individual characters intact, but they pro-nounced them in their original language. This meant that virtually all Chinese who were literate, regardless of their native tongue, could communicate with each other in writing, but not verbally.

This extraordinary factor was what made it possible for major elements of the primary Han [Chinese] culture to spread to the far reaches of the huge country. But the language diversity continued to divide the people into cultural enclaves that made the western regions of the country more difficult to rule.

Shortly after Mao Zedong and the Communist Party took over China in 1949 he took the extraordinary but commonsense step of decreeing that Mandarin, the language of the Beijing area of China, was to be the national language of the country, and mandated that it be taught in all elementary schools in the country. Now, most Chinese whose native tongue is not Mandarin are verbally bilingual.

The impact that the Chinese language has on the mind of the Chinese is far deeper and far more comprehensive than the influence of other languages on other people because the influence is both verbal and written.

All people who are not weaned on Chinese ideograms naturally react to both the sound and the written form of words in their own languages. But the reaction to words that are written with phonetic script is not nearly as strong as the reaction to pictorial ideograms that are representations of real things and explicit concepts.

Both the verbal and written forms of the Chinese language are therefore like massive software programs. They create and control the Chinese mind to a degree that goes well beyond the power of other languages.

This is the primary reasons why expatriate Chinese who have been out of China for several generations but have persevered in learning how to read and write Hanzi and speak the language continue to maintain their Chinese identity.

Becoming verbally fluent in Chinese and learning how to read and write some two thousand or more Hanzi is a major undertaking that requires intense study and practice for one to three years.

However, it is not necessary to become fluent in Chinese in order to gain a comprehensive understanding of Chinese culture. And many people who *do* become quite fluent in the language as far as speaking and understanding is concerned still do not have a total grasp of the culture.

That requires full knowledge of the meanings and nuances of several hundred key terms in the language—words that incorporate and reflect elements of the culture in the deepest sense—and is a separate challenge in itself.

These are the terms I refer to as "cultural code words" because they are pregnant with cultural meanings that go far beyond their one-dimensional surface meanings.

[2]

The Yin-Yang Principle
In Chinese Culture

I BELIEVE IT is impossible to fully understand Chin-ese attitudes and behavior without comprehensive knowledge of the ancient *yin-yang* principle in Chinese culture. The terms yin and yang are generally known around the world as relating to such opposites as hot-cold, sweet-sour, male-female, and positive-negative. But this view is incomplete.

The concept of yin and yang is, in fact, an explanation of the nature of the cosmos; of the behavior of all organic and inorganic material in the universe, as well as the invisible energy that infuses the cosmos down to the level of quantum physics.

The yin-yang concept incorporates the creation and extinction of all things in an unending cycle. It refers to the power that infuses all things in the cosmos and dictates that there must be—or should be—harmony between the positive and negative, the dark and the light, the active and the inactive, etc.

Several of the most basic elements of Chinese culture, including personal and business etiquette, are manifest-tations of the yin-yang principle, particularly the Chinese characteristic of thinking "in circles" in contrast to the "straight-line" thinking that prevails in the West.

Looking just below the surface of Chinese behavior reveals that the yin-yang principle applies to all relationships between males and females, between seniors and juniors, between the government and the private sector, in fact, to virtually all relationships and all act-ivities—including the food they eat and the order in which the dishes are consumed, and all of their traditional medical and therapeutic practices.

Chinese scholars and philosophers have been aware of and writing about the yin-yang principle—which could be defined as the interplay between opposites—since around 1,400 B.C. But long before this they had become acutely aware that the yin-yang relationships between things and people are not fixed, that they are in a constant state of flux, that they wax and wane in inverse proportions—between the hot and cold, the strong and the weak, the young and the old.

The personal and business etiquette of the Chinese is based on trying to keep all of the yin-yang relationships in harmony—which does not mean or infer equality in the relationships; only that the relationships are on a level that is acceptable, or bearable, to the parties concerned.

This view of human relations is not fair in the Western sense, but it is realistic in the sense that in nature equality is an absolute that can exist only in relative terms and for short periods of time.

Chinese culture is now evolving in the direction of Western cultures. The Chinese in the more industrialized areas of the country are giving preference to people-oriented standards that are making their society less formalistic, less ritualistic and less homogenous—and cer-tainly more human.

But in most areas of Chinese life, from the personal to the professional, the yin-yang principle is at play on some level, and it is generally necessary to understand what that means in terms of all relationships—especially business.

This is especially true for Americans and other Westerners who are programmed to view things as linear, and have poor vision—if any—of all of the things that are above, below and on the sides of that straight line.

In dealing successfully with the Chinese it is always vital to view the relationship—or proposed relationship—from a holistic viewpoint; being aware of and often taking into account these subtle and sometimes invisible elements.

Americans in particular typically regard this approach as somewhat irrational at best and obstructionist at worst, and begrudge taking the time necessary to deal with it. But investing the extra time generally cannot be avoided.

It is best to acknowledge the yin-yang principle upfront, and call it like it is in negotiations—emphasizing the positive and acknowledging the negative in order to achieve an acceptable agreement.

[3]
Dealing with Three Kinds of Logic in China

FEW THINGS more upsetting and confusing to Western executives, diplomats and globe-circling politicians—especially Americans—than trying to deal with people whose attitudes and behavior are not logical in the American sense of the word.

Even when Americans are knowledgeable enough to *know* that other people are not steeped in American style epistemology and logic they typically behave as if those they are dealing with should understand and accept their logical, rational point of view, and react accordingly.

This, of course, is a form of cultural blindness—or a willfully predatory nature—that is responsible for much of our misunderstanding and mishandling of business and diplomatic relations with other nations.

This cultural factor can be especially challenging in China, where there are three forms of logic: traditional Chinese logic, Communist logic and Western logic; and it is common for all three of these forms of logic to be at play in the same situation.

Even being aware of the existence of these three forms of logic and knowing something about them individually does not always make it easy to deal with the Chinese—a fact that the Chinese themselves are fully aware of, readily admit and take full advantage of.

Until the latter part of the 20th century Chinese in general were not allowed to behave in purely Western style logical ways, despite the fact that they could think logically in the Western sense in virtually all matters when they had a choice. The problem was they seldom had a choice.

This situation is further complicated in present-day China by the fact that people who have been educated and trained to think and behave logically in Western terms will often behave in the traditional Chinese way by choice or in the Communist way because they have no choice.

The traditional Chinese way of thinking is what I call "fuzzy logic," meaning that it is not the hard two-times-two-equals-four kind of thinking or straight-line thinking. It is "holistic" thinking, or thinking in circles, and in the

Chinese language is known as *buhe luoji de* (buu-hay luu-oh-jee duh).

Since few Westerners are experienced in holistic or circular thinking, Chinese attitudes and behavior are often confusing to them. But fuzzy thinking (the term was actually invented by an American) is often far more powerful than "straight-line" thinking because it is takes in a lot more territory in terms of time, space and long-term results.

Westerners dealing with the Chinese should prepare themselves by learning how to react to—and use—fuzzy logic, which means learning how to look at things in a far more comprehensive context than they commonly do. One of the things that *buhe luoji de* entails is making it necessary to take substantially more time to negotiate relationships and keep them on track.

Without intending to sell Americans and other Westerners short, we often come across as being concerned only about quick financial gain. That traditionally has not been the way of most Chinese—and Westerners who understand why the Chinese put long-term relationships before profit on the priority scale are much more likely to be welcomed in China.

[4]
The Importance of Connections in China

GUANXI (GWAHN-SHE), or "connections," is one of the most used and most important words in the Chinese vocabulary—and is a deeply embedded cultural phenol-menon that goes well beyond the Western concept of the term.

The role of *guanxi* in Chinese life naturally goes back to ancient times. From the dawn of China's civilization the people were controlled by beliefs, customs and laws that limited their ability to make personal and individual decisions. Virtually every aspect of their lives was pre-scribed, or was set by precedent, down to where they lived, what they wore, the work they did, the education they received, who they married, and how they interacted with other people.

Over the long millennia of Chinese history this system, supported and often required by imperial governments, became the foundation of the Chinese mindset.

In such a society the old adage "It's not what you know, it's who you know" becomes an axiom of life. Another obvious truism in this kind of society is the fact that it is generally not your intelligence, knowledge, ambition or motivation that determines you success in life; it is *guanxi,* the personal connections you have and how clever you are at using them.

Guanxi is usually translated into English as "con-nections," but this English term does not do justice to the cultural implications and importance of the word in Chinese society. In my book *China's Cultural Code Words* I explain the concept of *guanxi* by defining it as rela-tionships that are based on mutual dependence.

There is, of course, a certain amount of mutual de-pendence in all societies, but in the American mindset in particular mutual dependence is generally secondary to a strong sense of individualism and independence. Our mantra is that we take personal responsibility for our actions and our success or failure. Seeking and depending upon connections is not built into our way of life.

That is not the case in China. The essence of Chinese life, still today, is based on *guanxi*. The foreigner in China who attempts to get by without making and nurturing connections is almost always doomed to failure.

The personal as well as the professional lives of Chinese are based on making and keeping connections with a variety of people they can call on for help of one kind or another. Such *guanxi* are especially important in matters that involve government offices on any level.

The best approach to building up a network of connections is to start the process before your first visit to China, beginning with the obvious: the commercial attaché in the Chinese embassy in your country, your chambers of commerce in China, Chinese scholars and/or graduate Chinese students in a university near you, local Chinese companies that are involved in your area of interest, professional clubs with organizations in China, and so on.

Another obvious route for businesspeople in particular is to go to Hong Kong first, and begin your network building there, where possible contact avenues include banks, government offices, trading companies, attorneys and consultants.

Another important step: you must bone up on Chinese culture—both traditional and contemporary—because what you say in English must also make cultural sense in Chinese.

[5]
The Imperative of "Sincerity plus Understanding" in Chinese Culture

DEALING SUCCESSFULLY with the Chinese in business, diplomatic and political affairs requires an extraordinary level of knowledge about Chinese culture, from their day-to-day customs to their deepest beliefs and motivations.

As also noted in my book *China's Cultural Code Words*, understanding and dealing with commercial enterprises and government agencies in particular takes on an entirely new light when viewed from the Chinese perspective. Almost nothing follows the straightforward, expedient lines of thought and steps that logical and law-oriented Westerner expects.

Part of the difference in Chinese and Western thinking and behavior is expressed in the term *budan-xin* (boo-dahn-sheen), which means something like "sincerity plus understanding"—although I believe it would be more accurate to reverse these two concepts, with understanding coming first.

In its Chinese context, "understanding" refers to the out-sider understanding a situation from the Chinese perspective, to the depth and breadth that the Chinese do. And "sincerity" refers to the cultural requirement that the individual or individuals concerned conform completely to the expectations and standards of the Chinese way—that is, conforming to all of the personal, social and legal obligations that make up the foundation of Chinese thought and behavior.

In other words, in the Chinese context of things, a "sincere" person is one who can be depended upon to do what is right and expected from the Chinese viewpoint regardless of the situation.

This combination of understanding and sincerity in the Chinese context is the foundation of Chinese behavior, whether or not it makes sense to foreigners. And this is why the Chinese are continuously reminding foreigners that they must "understand" China in order to deal effectively with them.

It is also why the Chinese typically accuse foreigners of *not* understanding China when things go wrong. In the Chinese context of things, foreigners cannot be sincere in their relationships with Chinese if they do not understand China, since sincerity without understanding is impossible.

Like Americans (if I may make the comparison) the Chinese almost always automatically take the position that they are right and that their way of doing this should prevail. It is therefore very important for foreigners dealing with China to be aware of the *budan-xin* cultural factor and be prepared to deal with it.

I suggest that in the beginning of business or diplomatic relationships the foreigners involved note up-front to their Chinese counterparts that they are familiar with the role of *budan-xin* in Chinese culture because it is an integral part of their culture as well, and that there may be differences of opinion that require both sides to compromise for them to achieve their goals.

This will alert the Chinese to the fact that you do know something about China, and will provide you with a more solid footing for negotiating with them.

[6]
The Importance of Chinese Style "Unity" In Present-day China

ANOHER ASPECT of the Chinese mindset that foreigners should be aware of in order to deal with them more efficiently is expressed in the term *bi* (bee), which translates into English as unity—the condition of agreement; the combination of diverse beliefs and opinions into a whole.

On a philosophical level, this is an accurate description of the traditional Chinese concept of an ideal society. However, it is especially important for foreigners in China to be aware of the fact that this view of cultural unity as a national characteristic of the Chinese was never true, and that the contemporary role of *bi* is quite different from what this suggests.

Despite the influence of Buddhism and the teachings of Confucius and other sages who promoted harmonious, selfless relationships and unquestioning obedience to higher authority, the Chinese throughout their history have been extraordinarily independent-minded and primarily concerned about the survival and well-being of their nuclear and extended families.

Still today the values and loyalties of present-day Chinese tend to be first to the family, second to their work group in companies and to their communities in rural farm areas, and third to the individual.

While these three categories remain paramount in the day-to-day mindset and behavior of the typical Chinese, they are now also overlaid by extraordinarily strong feelings of patriotism and concern for the status of the country vis-à-vis the rest of the world.

There is a universal feeling among Chinese leaders and the people in general that they and their country have been discriminated against and vilified by other nationalities and nations for the last five hundred years, and they are unified in their efforts to reassert the image of themselves as an outstanding people and of China as a world leader

All foreigners dealing with China on any level for any purpose must keep these values, loyalties and feelings in mind in structuring and maintaining business, diplomatic and other relationships with the Chinese.

Unlike typical Americans whose motivations are primarily circumscribed by personal self-interest, the behavior of the Chinese is generally defined by the larger circle of obligations within the categories named above—obligations that color all of their relationships, and make dealing with them more complicated.

It regularly happens that what foreigners regard as logical and beneficial to individual Chinese as well as to the country at large does not meet the criteria of the people concerned—and these criteria differ according to the private or government position of the individuals involved.

Business and political relationships in China tend to be based on a series of personal factors rather than on mutual goodwill and mutual benefit and the kind and level of principles and facts that broadly speaking are the foundation of business and political practices in the West.

In other words, *bi* in its present-day context in China is based on first benefiting the Chinese groups and individuals concerned. Generally, the most effective way for foreigners to surmount this cultural barrier is to emphasize their desire to create a long-term relationship that will benefit both parties, making it possible for the relationship to continue well into the future *because* it is fair and balanced.

There is almost always a point in Chinese negotiations where pragmatism sets in and it is possible to structure a relationship that is equitable. But persistence, often over an extended period of time, is essential.

[7]
The Subtle and often Insidious Role Of Gongei in China

THERE ARE MANY words in the Chinese language that are designed and used to show respect and deference to the elderly and superiors, to acknowledge social inferiority as well as demonstrate social superiority, to indicate sex and age differences, to account for extended-family relationships, to seek favors, and so on.

This extensive vocabulary is a result of the vital importance that personal relationships have had in China since ancient times—which in turn resulted in people becoming extraordinarily sensitive to and about all of their relationships.

One of the most interesting, deceptive and powerful of these key words is the term *gongwei* (goong-way-ee), or "flattery." The extraordinarily precise etiquette that traditionally controlled the lives of the Chinese and the extreme sensitivity that resulted from this etiquette gave birth to the extreme use of flattery.

With both success and survival generally depending on maintaining good relations with others, especially those who were higher on the social ladder and the authorities—

again in the extreme sense—the use of flattery became a national custom that was raised to a fine art.

The use of *gongwei* is still deeply embedded in the character and personality of the Chinese, and has become one of their most valuable tools in dealing with foreigners.

The Chinese learned a long time ago that Westerners—Americans in particular—are especially susceptible to flattery, and they use it with great skill in disarming and manipulating them.

Much of this flattery is rather innocuous and can be passed off as courtesy or expressions of goodwill. And that is fine as long as the situations are personal and there are no other motives behind the custom.

But that is often not the case, even in situations that do not appear to the outsider to have any hidden agendas.

Of course, it is common practice in all cultures to flatter someone if you want something from them. But there are often additional ramifications in China that go beyond minor or simple favors.

The Chinese use of *gongwei* in business and in politics has been raised to a high level—to the point that it often becomes the primary factor in achieving goals, especially when the relationships or negotiations involve Westerns who are not accustomed to basing their presentations on flattery.

The point to beware of is that in many if not most of these cases the intent of the Chinese side is to gain more than an equitable advantage in the relationships.

As is always the case in all cross-cultural interactions with the Chinese [and all others for that matter] the best offense as well as defense is to know as much as possible about their mindset and the tactics they use in dealing with each other and with foreigners.

This advice especially applies to *gongwei* because it appears so sincere, so non-threatening. It is not easy for many people to discern the difference between honest, sincere praise that is deserved, and flattery designed to gain an edge.

[8]
To Survive and Thrive in China You Must Have Mianzi

UNTIL THE LAST two decades of the 20th century it was difficult for ordinary Chinese to develop a strong sense of self-esteem or pride because the culture in which they lived denied them the right to think and act independently and generally prevented them from being able to demonstrate their own individual worth, including taking credit for personal accomplishments.

Failure to abide by these ancient taboos—many of which had been codified as law by the Imperial dynasties and continued by the Communist regime—was regarded as immoral and unethical by traditional standards, and could have series consequences.

However, there were two key ways in China that individuals could stand out quietly and unobtrusively. One of these ways was for them to develop a non-threatening skill in an art or craft or another endeavor to an extraordinary degree—and that is exactly what many Chinese did over the generations.

One other way the Chinese were able to feel good about themselves without breaking any taboos—and by far the most important—was to have *mianzi* (me-enn-jee) or "face"—meaning to have unblemished reputations for living up to all of the cultural expectations that had built up over the centuries, and most importantly, to not allow anyone to damage their face or themselves damage anyone else's face unless they were prepared to take the consequences, since such behavior called for a reciprocal action of some kind.

Having "face" was generally more important than having some kind of special expertise, since economic and social survival in traditional China depended upon not having any serious blemishes on one's reputation that would prevent one from making and keeping the kind of "social connections" that were essential for survival in an authoritarian hierarchical society.

Now, for the first time in their history, private Chinese are mostly free to pursue individual goals, to take pride in their accomplishments, and to otherwise act as individuals. But the importance of social connections and "face" have hardly diminished.

To be successful in business you still have to protect your "face" and develop an extensive network of personal connections with local and regional government officials and with your suppliers and customers—and without similar social connections your personal life as well is not likely to go smoothly.

This need for *mianzi* and connections is one of the first things that foreigners wanting to succeed in China must learn, and once the lesson is taken to heart they must thereafter spend a substantial amount of time and expense in maintaining their "face" and their connections.

The Chinese concept of "face" is very personal, and covers any act, comment, tone of voice or even facial expression that indicates criticism or disapproval. Because of this extraordinary sensitivity, foreign managers should be cautious about criticizing or disciplining employees in public. Public criticism of the government is especially taboo.

There are a variety of things involved in developing and maintaining "face" and connections in China, many of which are familiar to most people—eating and drinking together, giving gifts, doing favors, not criticizing people to their face, and so on. But these things must be done according to the cultural protocol that applies, or such efforts may backfire.

For one thing, it is fairly common for Chinese in all social categories to take personal advantage of those who need their friendship and cooperation, especially naïve foreigners—and these situations may be hard for foreigners to recognize and avoid, but it is vital that you know how to handle them.

Throughout China's history, including the heyday of the Communist regime, many bureaucrats made a regular practice of using their power to get personal favors for themselves or members of their families from people who needed their services—and the practice continues today. It is even more important to know how to handle these situations when government officials are concerned.

If you encounter such situations and are not that familiar with Chinese culture the best recourse is to get insights and guidance from a trusted Chinese friend or from other foreigners who have been in China for many years, are well-versed in the intricacies of business and personal relationships, and can guide you around the pitfalls.

The Chinese appreciate it when foreigners take a sincere interest in their traditional culture, and will invariably go out of their way to enlighten and help new-comers.

[9]
The "Back Door" Approach
To Business and Political Success!

IN CHINA WHERE personal connections play a paramount role in all relationships—business, personal and political—the typical Western way of doing things is often ineffective, and may be considered both arrogant and rude.

Historically ordinary Chinese had no inalienable rights to protect them from those in power. Bureaucracy was universal and honed to perfection, and expecting something simply because it was "right" and you should get it, and especially "demanding" something or some action, would virtually always result in doors being slammed in your face—or far more serious results.

This situation resulted in the Chinese, including government officials, having to develop a variety of strategies and tactics to get things done—ways that were unofficial but were a key part of the system—like authorities allowing a black market to function because it provided them with advantages of one kind or another, including keeping the level of frustration in the population below the point of eruption.

After the Communist Party came to power in China in 1949 and instituted a number of democratic principles and polices—including giving women the right to vote—the policy of both allowing and promoting unofficial processes remained virtually unchanged, both because it was so deeply embedded in the culture and because it continued to serve the interests of the government.

The most common of these unofficial practices was using the *hou men* (hoe-uu mane) or "back door"—that is, contacting and making deals with people behind-the-scenes, in private settings, making them *fait accompli* on the QT.

Despite political reforms and cultural changes that have made life in China far more open, rational and practical, the use of *hou men* remains a vital part of the conduct of business, national politics and international relationships.

When there is a "back door" most Chinese will automatically take it—and if there isn't one they will generally attempt to make one, because that is almost always the fastest and most efficient way of getting official as well as unofficial things done.

In simple terms, these "back doors" are people who can get things done because of their power positions or because they can call on their personal relationships with others to bypass bureaucracy, official policies and often laws as well.

Obviously, this aspect of personal as well public behavior is a factor in all cultures, but in China the *hou men* element functions as an integral part of business and politics, without which the official social, economic and political systems would not work well enough to sustain themselves.

Until foreigners who are newly arrived in China learn about the existence of *hou men* and develop skill in making and using them their chances of success are slim.

In fact, it pays to start building "back door" connections before you set foot in China—developing contacts and getting introductions through the overseas offices of Chinese companies, chambers of commerce, banks, cultural organizations, university professors, such clubs as Kiwanis, and so on.

[10]
Virtue vs. the Law
in Chinese Culture

ONE OF MY favorite pieces of Confucian philosophy is: "Attempting to rule people by laws that require them to act the same leads to resentment and disobedience of the laws and to feel no shame!"

Confucius believed that people should behave because of the virtue that is or should be inherent in all human beings; not because of manmade laws—a precept that is wonderful in its optimistic view of human nature, but often unworkable in reality.

On the surface, the Imperial rulers of China appeared to take part of this philosophy to heart because many of China's *falu* (fah-luu) or "laws" were not codified or published. It was left up to judges, officials and policemen to decide on what was legal and not legal; on what was allowed and what could be punished.

China's early Communist leaders followed the Imperial pattern to some extent. In present-day China there are still unpublished laws as well as many that are published but retain some of the essence of Confucius by being worded vaguely—so vaguely in many cases that their purpose cannot be clearly understood.

Like the emperors before them, China's Communist leaders know that if the laws are vague and punishments are quick and severe most people will refrain from doing anything that might even seem to be illegal.

However, in a slight bow toward realism, if most people ignored certain laws—old or new—the government sometimes pretended they didn't exist; or said that they were just a test.

Still today the government prefers to rule by general directives rather than codified and published laws, which often puts foreign businesspeople and others at a disadvantage because they cannot anticipate how the directives are going to be interpreted.

China's constitution, amended in 2004, states that the "freedom of the people" is guaranteed and "the personal dignity of citizens is inviolable."
It also states the families and work unit of individuals who are arrested must be notified with 24 hours.

While this new amendment resulted in thousands of people being released from prison, it has since typically been ignored when it concerns political activists. Non-judicial panels of police and local civil authorities can sentence people to prison-like labor camps for up to three years—or to high-security psychiatric facilities for the criminally insane.

Citizens also have the constitutional right to represent themselves in court proceedings as well as to be represented by attorneys. But in politically sensitive cases the accused typically are allowed to see their attorneys only once before hearings. These trials usually last for only a few hours, sentences are usually handed down immediately—and when the sentence is death executions often follow within days.

Public security in China is buttressed by a vast army of agents, informers and spies. Using frequent household checks, local police stations keep a record of all marriages, divorces, the birth of children, deaths, where people work, and residential changes. People over the age of 16 are required to carry identity cards.

Security agents also keep tabs on foreigners living in and visiting China, with periodic checks of hotels. Bribery of one kind or another, including kickbacks, is endemic in China, and security people appear to keep especially close watch on foreigners and Chinese employees of foreign companies.

Foreign businesspeople and foreign visitors are advised to be cautious about behaving in a suspicious manner as well as talking about politics and religion. The best approach for foreigners is to get the advice of Chinese friends and partners when in doubt about any activity.

Although the Chinese naturally view virtue [*shanliang / shawn-lee-ung*] in its Chinese setting it encompasses many of the characteristics that were eventually to become the basis for the highest level of humanistic thought in the West.

[11]
Bartering "Social Credits" In China

IN SOCIETIES THAT do not have laws governing the way people to deal with each other in relationships—business, personal, political, etc.—the relationships must be based on trade-offs of one kind or another.

This system, which prevailed in China until recent times, opens the door for those who are in positions of power to take advantage of those who are less privileged, and makes it imperative that people in general become skilled in developing and maintaining relationships that are based on arbitrary factors rather than principles of honesty, fairness, and so on.

Of course, this system automatically disadvantages ordinary people who must deal with government officials, and it complicates the lives of business owners and managers and trades people on all social and economic levels.

While China traditionally had customs, government edicts and laws that pertained to behavior, all of these things combined did not constitute a comprehensive body of restraints or provisions that provided formal or official guidelines for commercial and political activities.

This circumstance—which primarily grew out of the philosophies of Lao-Tse and Confucius, China's best known 5th and 6th century B.C. sages—made it imperative that the Chinese develop a practical way of handling their day-to-day affairs, both personal and professional, and they did this by a process that came to be known as *bao* (bah-oh), which may be translated as "social reciprocity." I also refer to it as "bartering social credits."

Despite the fact that the younger generations of Chinese, especially those with international educations, are gradually breaking away from the restraints of *bao* in order to deal more effectively with foreigners, the use of "social credits" continues to play an important role in all aspects of life and work in China.

It is still advisable for foreigners assigned to China to build up *bao* with business contacts and government officials as rapidly and as widely as possible. Just as in the U.S. and elsewhere, one of the primary ways of building up *bao* in China is hosting dinner and drinking parties.

The Chinese are famous for their banquet parties, which are typically extraordinary demonstrations of the traditional culture—from relationships among family members, friends and professional contacts, to indulging themselves in pleasuring the eyes, the palate and the stomach.

[12]
The Role of the "Force"
In China

UNTIL THE DEATH of Mao Zedong in 1976 and the emergence of Deng Xiaoping as the paramount leader of China a short time later, most Chinese lived in what an ancient sage referred to as the "bitter sea"—a reference to the natural hardships they confronted in their efforts to survive as well as the oppressive customs and laws imposed upon them over the millennia by the ruling elite.

The philosophical and political restraints under which the Chinese had lived since ancient times denied them the right to think and behave independently; to follow their instincts and their dreams.

When the pragmatic Deng Xiaoping freed the Chinese from these ancient chains it unleashed a kind and level of energy never before experienced in the country—the same phenomenon that had occurred earlier in Japan, Taiwan and Korea and resulted in these nations becoming economic powerhouses.

In less than decade the unleashed ambitions and energy of millions of Chinese had transformed the eastern seaboard and some of the nearer central regions of the country. This process is still underway, and there is concern about what direction it will take because the power of China's armed forces is keeping pace with its industrial growth. The armed forces are, in fact, leaders in the industrialization of the country, owning hundreds of corporations outright and controlling many others.

There is some fear that China could follow in the footsteps of Japan, which industrialized in a fifteen-year period beginning in 1870, transformed itself into a Western-style military power in the process, defeated the Russians in 1904-05, and soon afterward invaded and conquered Korea.

By the early 1930s the Japanese military had taken full control of the government, and began a campaign to colonize all of Asia, if not the world. Thwarted in that attempt, the Japanese turned their own newly unleashed spirit and energy to becoming the second largest economic power in the world in less than thirty years after their defeat in World War II—a truly remarkable accomplishment for a tiny warrior-dominated agricultural country that had been closed to the outside world from the 1630s to the 1850s.

Unlike the Japanese, however, the Chinese have never been so driven to militarily control all of Asia or the world, but since ancient times they had envisioned themselves as the "Central Kingdom" with those around them as tributaries.

It cannot be said that present-day Chinese, on any level, aim to reassert their position as the Central Kingdom. But the force that drives them is not held back by the philosophical restraints that have kept the United States from following the ancient pattern of colonialism.

China will continue to grow and become more powerful not only to protect itself but because the ambitions and desires of its billion-plus people have not yet been fulfilled.

Nations that do not quickly learn how to interact effectively with China on equitable terms could soon become tributary states to the Central Kingdom—an incredible reprise of history that is already well under way, gaining momentum daily and spreading beyond Asia.

***

If you see in any given situation only what
everybody else can see, you can be said to
be so much a representative of your
culture that you are a
victim of it.

—S. I. Hayakawa—

***

JAPAN

[1]
The Imperative of Harmony
In the Japanese Way

THE FIRST LAW in Japan's first Constitution, promulgated in the 7th century, stated that *wa* [wah] or "harmony" was to be the foundation of all human relationships...a concept that was the foundation of Shintō, the native religion of the Japanese.

From that era on, all elements of Japanese culture and society were generally structured on the basis of maintaining social class, hierarchy and order in all relationships...something that did not treat people as equals or ensure equal opportunity or the Western concept of human rights.

When Japan emerged as the second largest economy in the world in less than 30 years following the destruction of World War II the Japanese repeatedly attributed their incredible accomplishment to *wa*...to the harmonious relationships that existed on every level of their society.

There were other reasons for this success, but the elements making up the Japanese cultural concept of *wa* played a primary role—despite the fact that there were many negative factors in this ancient concept.

One of the most conspicuous of these negative elements is the still virtually absolute requirement for maintaining

Japanese style harmony among members of work units as well as with employees in other sections and departments of companies and organizations.

Japanese *wa* is based on the concept that individuals should not say or do anything that would embarrass or hurt the feelings of others, including such things as praising and/or rewarding fellow co-workers for their personal accomplishments.

This reason for this element is that bringing attention to the performance of one individual in a group contravenes the group-comes-first custom that has long been institutionalized and ritualized in Japanese culture.

This aspect of Japanese culture is especially rampant in education, where outstanding individuals who would like to eliminate obviously deleterious practices and replace them with better methods are typically outvoted by fellow teachers and administrators.

As late as 2007 when a number of corporate engineers and scientists insisted on being recognized and compensated for their outstanding technological breakthroughs and scientific discoveries their actions became national news and caused heated debates nationwide.

However, last fall a professional association took it upon itself to breach this cultural barrier by recognizing the accomplishments of one of its members, without any apparent negative feedback—a noteworthy change in Japanese behavior.

In any event, the plus side of the traditional group-orientation of Japanese culture obviously outweighs the bad when taken as a whole—despite the ongoing frustration caused by individuals having to suppress their own feelings as well as forego obviously worthwhile measures on behalf of *wa*.

Foreigners interacting with the Japanese on any level for any purpose must be aware of and to some extent follow the tenets of Japanese style harmony in order to succeed.

[2]

The Cultural Molds
that Created and Control
the Traditional Japanese Mindset

MANY PEOPLE around the world are familiar with the Japanese term *kata* (kah-tah) from its use in the martial arts, where it describes the forms or processes used in training. But *kata* are far more important to understanding and dealing with the Japanese than this martial arts connection implies.

The whole of Japan's traditional culture, from personal etiquette to how one learned to do all of the routine things in life, were based on precise *kata*—on precisely prescribed ways of doing them.

There was a way of eating (tabe-kata), a way of walking (aruki-kata), a way of thinking (kangae-kata), a way of reading (yomi-kata), a way of writing (kaki-kata), a way of talking (hanashi-kata), a way of doing things in general (yari-kata), and so on across the entire spectrum of human behavior.

In earlier times the interjection of personal preference or deviation for any reason from these prescribed *kata* was both immoral and unethical from the viewpoint of Japanese culture. Failure to follow the prescribed *kata* invariably had an immediate and sometimes fatal effect.

Failure to bow properly to a samurai warrior, for example, could get one shortened by a head. There was a shogunate edict which said that a samurai could kill anyone on the spot who failed to follow the prescribed forms of behavior. This edict was known as *kirisute-gomen!* (kee-ree-suu-tay go-mane), figuratively "kill-by your leave," or "kill-pardon me." In effect in meant to kill, say "pardon me" and walk away.

This prescribed and enforced conformity to exact ways of doing things had a profound influence on the character and personality of the Japanese, making them homogenous to an extraordinary degree as well as predictable, because everybody was taught and trained to think and do things the same way.

The *kata* concept in the arts and crafts was also responsible for the remarkable manual skills that have long been typical of the Japanese, for their ability to focus on things with great intensity, and their compulsion to "get things right."

I became acutely aware of the presence and role of *kata* in Japanese culture in the 1950s and began to write about it but it was not until 1990 that I put the whole thing together in a book first published as *THE KATA FACTOR – Japan's Secret Weapon.*

Shortly after the book came out in a Japanese edition I was asked to address an assembly of some 400 Japanese businesspeople and scholars. I was astounded to learn that the Japanese themselves had never looked at or discussed the role of individual *kata* in their culture.

They were so kata-ized in their thinking and behavior that the idea of analyzing their behavior with individual *kata* as the starting point had apparently not occurred to anyone.

They were, however, acutely aware of the effect that *kata* had on their thinking and behavior, and continuously pointed to the fact that they had one of the world's most homogenized culture. But they did not attribute this specifically to the overall effect of *kata.*

In the large group I addressed only one individual took exception to my explanation of the Japanese way of thinking and doing things. This grey-haired distinguished looking gentleman stood up and said:

"Everything Mr. De Mente said about Japanese culture is wrong! The essence of Japanese character and behavior is derived from Shintō! He does not mention Shintō at all!"

I knew instantly that the gentleman [who turned out to be Japan's premiere Shintō authority] had not read the book thoroughly because I did bring out the role and importance of Shintō in Japanese culture.

Still today no one can fully understand and appreciate the typical attitudes and behavior of the Japanese without knowledge of the *kata* that created their mindset and continues to control their behavior to a remarkable degree.

While the legal and social sanctions against ignoring traditional *kata* are no longer life-threatening, they are nevertheless severe in modern terms.

In business and all other professional relationships failure to follow the traditionally prescribed behavior can have all kinds of repercussions, from an employee not being promoted, or being sent to a workplace in the boonies, to relationships being terminated.

In the meantime, I have updated the book and it has been republished as *KATA – The Key to Understanding & Dealing with the Japanese* [Tuttle Publishing].

[3]
The Japanese Language
As a Cultural Obstacle

LANGUAGES ARE, of course, the medium of thought and communication and are therefore the reservoir as well as the vehicle of culture. The older and more exclusive a culture the more the language both programs and controls the thinking and behavior of a people.

The Japanese language is both ancient and different from all other languages. This results in the traditional Japanese mindset and way of doing things being unique.

What this means is that the words that make up the Japanese language do not mean the same thing as their equivalents in other languages. Both their cultural connotations and use differ to varying degrees.

In other words, *wa* [wah], the Japanese word for harmony, means *Japanese style* harmony, which differs significantly from the meaning and use of the English word harmony when spoken by native English speakers.

Wa in its Japanese context refers to conforming to the Japanese way of thinking and doing things, from personal social etiquette and customs to interpersonal and professional relationships—the things that make the Japanese *Japanese.*

Not only do Japan's "culturally pregnant" words differ from their foreign equivalents in meaning and use, there are also different "levels" of Japanese that might be described as low level, informal and formal. These levels are distinguished by different vocabulary as well as word endings that change their nuance and their use.

In other words, there are what might loosely be called three Japanese dialects, each with its own vocabulary and word endings. Furthermore, the informal and formal versions of these different modes of speech have a feminine mode and a masculine mode.

While the use of the formal level of Japanese has diminished significantly since the late 1900s, as has the "low level," all of the three modes continue to play a role communication in Japan.

It is possible to express yourself fully and completely in informal, "common" Japanese, but there are numerous occasions when formal speech is required by the prevailing standards and etiquette.

To communicate "properly" in Japanese—that is be culturally correct—requires knowledge of both the informal and formal levels of the language, and be skilled in using them.

Today, broadly speaking, most Japanese have not mastered the formal level of the language, and it is common to hire or otherwise arrange for people who are skilled in this level to make speeches, presentations and other types of discourse when formal language is desired or required.

Fortunately, the Japanese are well aware of the character of their language and the demands it makes on people, and do not expect foreigners to know or use the formal level of the language even though they may be quite fluent in the informal level. There are, however, a growing number of foreigners in Japan who *have* mastered the formal level of the language, and they both surprise and impress their Japanese audiences.

The point of this is that foreigners interacting with Japanese who do not speak English [or other foreign language] and have not been exposed to the culture of the foreigner concerned should be aware that what they say and how they say it may not be understood or accepted by the Japanese.

This is made more important by the fact that the Japanese typically say they understand and accept when they do not—out of embarrassment or shame and/or a desire not to upset or disappoint the foreign speaker.

This means that it is often necessary for you to repeat yourself several times; make your key points in different ways; and continuously ask you Japanese counterparts questions that will reveal whether or not they understand.

The number of foreigners who have made presentations and cut deals in Japan and went home thinking everything was settled are too numerous to count.

Regardless of their level of understanding the Japanese expect continuing contact and dialogue with their foreign partners. When the foreign side does not continue regular contact the Japanese will generally proceed on their own, doing things their way.

This invariably means that somewhere down the road—usually between two and three years—the two sides are so far apart that the relationship must be renegotiated; or the foreign side simply opts out.

[4]
"Indulgent Love" in Japanese Relationships and Management

ONE OF THE most powerful elements in Japan's traditional culture is subsumed in the word *amae* (ah-my), which incorporates the fundamental principle underlying the traditional, idealized behavior of the Japanese, and although significantly weakened by cultural changes that have been going on in Japan in modern times, especially since the mid-1900s, it is still a vital factor in the overall mindset of the Japanese.

Amae, from the verb *amaeru* (ah-my-rue), refers to presuming upon the love and indulgence of others when speaking or behaving in a manner that will cause some level of inconvenience, irritation or some other form of friction...and not expecting any negative feedback.

To react properly to expressions or actions of *amae* requires that individuals repress all of their selfish instincts and behave toward others as mothers to toward beloved children—treating them honestly, generously and kindly, regardless of the circumstances.

In this idealized *amae*-based world of early Japan the golden rule was that people should be able to depend upon each other without fear of being cheated, disadvantaged or embarrassed in any way. In other words, *amae* incorporated the concepts of absolute dependence and absolute trust in all human relations.

Of course, this *amae* morality was never practiced perfectly in Japan at any time, but it was sufficiently powerful to permeate the culture and to raise the standards of behavior of ordinary people in Japan well above the average found in other countries.

The inculcation of the *amae* principle in Japanese began to wane following the end of World War II in 1945, but its influence is still felt, even in the younger generations. Older people simply cannot feel at ease with others until they have developed an *amae*-type relationship with them.

This is still true today, especially in business relationships, and is one of the reasons why it generally takes longer to establish business ties in Japan than in Western countries. It is also the reason why many of the actions of Japanese are based on personal factors, rather than the "hard facts" espoused by Western businesspeople.

I introduced the concept of *amae* to Western businessmen as a vital factor in the attitudes and behavior of the Japanese in my book *Japanese Etiquette & Ethics in Business*, first published in 1959, and as of this writing still in print [in its 8th edition] at McGraw-Hill.

In that book I wrote that *amae* can be translated figuratively as "indulgent love," and that it was the pillar around which the traditional character, personality and aspirations of the Japanese were built.

The principle and practice of *amae* are certainly not unique to Japan, but the Japanese were apparently the only people (other than perhaps isolated tribes) who made it the primary essence of their social system.

Many Western businesspeople who began visiting Japan from the 1960s on became fascinated by the *amae* concept but they had extreme difficulty in attempting to conduct themselves in an *amae* manner when dealing with their Japanese partners and suppliers.

Growing up in Western societies has traditionally been related to *repressing* the need for *amae* and its use as a tactic or ploy in dealing with other people. In the Western context, achieving adulthood means leaving most *amae* thoughts and behavior behind, in one's childhood.

However, Westerner businesspeople who became familiar with the *amae* concept from 1960 on were, in fact, able to improve their relationships with their Japanese contacts because they better understood the cultural rationale of their behavior. But this familiarity did not end all of the friction and misunderstandings between Westerners and their Japanese partners.

The power of *amae* in Japanese culture—both in business and in private relationships—has noticeably diminished but it is still the ideal foundation for all relationships in Japan, and must be understand and dealt with in order to create and maintain the harmony that is required by the society.

In recent years it has become fairly common to see the word *amae* in Western books, magazines and in the news media in reference to Japanese attitudes and behavior, and remarkably, some of the changes that have occurred in the Western approach to personnel management are based on *amae* principles.

The adoption of some elements of *amae* in corporate behavior in the United States in particular—in the 1970s and 80s—was a direct result of the rise of Japan as an economic superpower. These elements, expressed in different terms, included a much more personal and employee-oriented approach to management.

[5]
Creating and Sustaining Relationships in Japan

THE ETIQUETTE SYSTEM that began evolving in the earliest period of Japan's history was to become what was probably the most comprehensive, the most precise and the most rigidly enforced forms of behavior in any society, before or since.

During the long and culturally defining era of the Tokugawa Shogunate [1603-1867] Japanese etiquette was refined down to the point that the rules for presenting gifts to high officials covered over 200 pages—and failure to follow them precisely could have serious consequences.

By the beginning of the 1800s the national etiquette had become so structured, refined and sophisticated that a simple carpenter sent to England in the late 1800s to build a teahouse for a London banker was mistaken for a member of Japan's royal family when he presented himself at the banker's home.

Until the mid-1900s all Japanese, on all levels of society, were physically trained and verbally taught to behave in the prescribed manner. There was no question about whether or not the young, from infancy on, would be trained in etiquette or how they would be trained to behave. It was in integral part of the lifestyle—of being Japanese.

In earlier times, not behaving in the prescribed manner was a serious fault that could get one ostracized, if not eliminated. As mentioned in a previous column, during the last centuries of the Tokugawa period not behaving properly toward a samurai could get one killed on the spot.

The first Westerners to show up in Japan in the 1540s noted that the behavior of the typical Japanese was the kind one might, in fact, expect of royalty. The higher the rank of an individual, the more detailed the prescribed manner of behavior, and the more rigorous the behavior was enforced.

Etiquette in today's Japan is not nearly as comprehensive or as strictly enforced as it was prior to the introduction of democracy into the country from 1946 on, but it remains far more detailed and important in the daily behavior of adults than manners in most other countries.

Most young Japanese are, in fact, no longer trained in the traditional forms of behavior, but many of the old forms of etiquette are still followed by adults, particularly in formal situations. The young who do not learn the prevailing standards of behavior by absorption as they grow up are typically required by their employers to attend etiquette classes and pass tests, particularly if they are employed by government agencies and larger companies.

One major aspect of the Japanese etiquette system is covered by the term *aisatsu* [ay-sot-sue], which translates as "greeting" and "salutation," and still today the rules and forms involved in *aisatsu* are especially important personally, in business, and in politics.

There are several times during the year that businesspeople and politicians are expected to make personal, formal visits to the offices, shops or factories of their contacts—to pay their respects those who are important to them in their business or professional lives by bowing and stating formal institutionalized expressions.

These visits include occasions when congratulations are in order and when thanking individuals for their past support and/or patronage and asking them to continue favoring you.

The most important season for making *aisatsu* visits to customers, suppliers, supporters and people in power positions [government officials, corporate executives, etc.] is during the first week after New Year's Day.

The Westerner who really wants to "fit in" in Japan should learn a number of the more important forms of *aisatsu*, such as the formal greetings that take place in the business world during New Year's and on other auspicious occasions, from weddings to funerals. [See my *Etiquette Guide to Japan—Know the Rules that Make the Difference;* also: *Japan Unmasked—The Character and Culture of the Japanese,* and: *Japan's Cultural Code Words—233 Key Terms that Explain the Attitudes and Behavior of the Japanese.*]

[6]
NEMAWASHI
One of the Secrets of
Doing Business in Japan

THE CULTURAL requirements of *wa* [wah], or "harmony," in all areas of traditional Japanese society fundamentally influenced the use of the language as well as the interactions between individuals and groups.

This influence included the choice of words and word-endings, depending on the age, gender and the relationship of the individuals involved and the nature of the interactions. This resulted in the development of feminine forms of speech, male forms of speech, and a "respect" form—all of which became deeply embedded in the culture.

The imperative of maintaining Japanese-style harmony played an especially important role in business and political decisions, since both could have far-ranging affects on individuals and large numbers of people, as well as on the business enterprises and the political institutions involved.

This gave birth to the development of a behind-the-scenes process that made it possible for people to avoid public embarrassment and possible failure by achieving consensus before going public with decisions—a process that came to be known as *nemawashi* (nay-mah-wah-she).

Nemawashi literally means "root revolving," and originally referred to spreading out the roots of plants being transplanted so they would be more stable, get more moisture, and grow better. In its new business, political and social meaning *nemawashi* refers to discreet lobbying Japanese style.

Most *nemawashi* activities, often on a one-on-one basis, eventually encompasse all the key people who would be concerned with or involved in implementing any decision made. It is both a sounding board for testing the response to an idea without exposing anyone to risk, as well as a lobbying mechanism used by an individual or group wanting to get something approved by the group, company, or other organization.

Using the *nemawashi* process effectively requires considerable knowledge of Japanese culture in general—especially with interpersonal relationships within the structure of the company concerned. Failure to involve people who feel they should have been included, or bringing in people who are unacceptable to the others involved, for whatever reason, can sabotage the effort.

The importance of the *nemawashi* practice in Japan should not be underestimated. The group mentality and group commitment that has prevailed in Japanese society for centuries still dominates the thinking and behavior of most Japanese, and is built into the management systems of all but a few maverick companies.

By Western standards, extraordinary patience is generally required to develop a relationship with a Japanese company. Once an agreement is reached, however, initiating a new program often moves swiftly because the *nemawashi* process has made all of the key people aware of what it is all about and what they are supposed to do.

Business publications, consultants and a growing number of people around the world who are directly involved with Japan are familiar with the term *nemawashi*, and some of them, particularly those who are stationed in Japan or visit there, use the term regularly.

Of course, various forms of *nemawashi* are used in other countries, but generally it is not as precise or as formally institutionalized and ritualized as it is in Japan.

I believe the term should be formally adopted for general use around the world because it subsumes a broad spectrum of the elements that go into establishing and maintaining positive, constructive relationships in all personal as well as professional settings.

While American businesspeople in the 1980s adopted a number of the more rational and practical Japanese management and manufacturing processes [in order to keep from being colonized by Japan] they ignored the lessons they should have learned from Japan's meltdown in the early 1990s.

Instead, in the mid-1990s American business executives as well as bureaucrats and politicians adopted the traditional Japanese preference for circumstantial policies over solid principles—a disastrous move that was responsible for the meltdown of the American economy in 2008...and could end up having similar results in China.

[7]
Japan's Do-or-Die
Cultural Syndrome!

JAPAN'S FAMED FEUDAL era samurai warriors [the elite class that developed in the 12th century and ruled the country until 1870] left their imprint on the culture of the country in every aspect and area of Japanese thought and behavior—an imprint that still today is discernible in the character and personality of the Japanese.

In the exclusive samurai class the mental and physical training of male children was well under way by the time they reached their seventh birthday. They became full-fledged samurai warriors on their 15th birthday.

In addition to training in the use of the sword and other weapons, they were trained to obey their lords without question, to be courageous in battle well beyond the norm for ordinary soldiers, to carefully groom themselves every morning before going out in public, and to be extra-ordinarily diligent in everything else they set out to do.

They were also trained in the mental and physical discipline necessary for them to commit a painful form of suicide if ordered to do so by their lords or by the feudal authorities.

As the centuries passed the training style and mindset of the samurai gradually seeped into the attitudes and behavior of the common people, resulting in the typical Japanese being extraordinarily concerned about appear-ance, extraordinarily diligent about learning the skills of their particular trade (or activity of any kind), continuously trying to improve themselves, and refusing to accept fail-ure.

This mindset led to the extraordinary importance and use of the word *ganbaru* (gahn-bah-ruu), which means to persevere, to persist, to never give up (also sometimes written in English letters with an "m" as *gambaru* / gahm-bah-ruu).

At all times in all things that were demanding to any degree, the Japanese were continuously admonished, en-couraged and expected to *gambatte!* (gahm-baht-tay!)—to do their best; to not give up no matter what the odds.

The concept of *gambaru*-ing eventually became so deeply embedded in the psyche of the Japanese that it was equated with being a true or real Japanese. In military situations in particular, not persevering to the very last breath of life was considered seriously shameful to the whole country.

Still today *gambatte!* *[do your best!]* and *gambarimasho* (gahm-bah-ree-mah-show!) [Let's do our absolute best!] are two of the most used words and phrases in the vocabulary of the Japanese.

They are used in work situations, in sports, in learning any kind of skill, and especially in any kind of competitive activity. In recent times Olympic athletes have been threatened with death when they failed to *ganbaru* and win their events.

I do not recommend that other people adopt this extreme approach to cultural training and day-to-day behavior, but some Americans and other Westerners could definitely benefit from a heavy dose of it.

If businesspeople, diplomats and others who deal with Japan are not familiar with this aspect of Japanese culture they are likely to be seriously disadvantaged because it leads them to underestimate the Japanese and not extend their own best efforts.

The *ganbaru* syndrome is far more kata-ized [meaning institutionalized and ritualized] in Japanese behavior than similar cultural conditioning is in Western cultures, where there is almost always an out if you make a good show of having done your best. Traditionally there were no "outs" in the samurai class on in the later military forces.

Another important aspect of the *ganbaru* syndrome in business and diplomatic situations is that it is often so subtle, so below the surface and typically camouflaged with a variety of delaying tactics, that the inexperienced Westerner often does not understand what is going on.

Westerners who are not thoroughly experienced in the ins-and-outs of how and why the Japanese think and behave the way they do would do well to acquaint themselves with the *kata* (kah-tah), the cultural "molds" that shaped and continue to control the mindset and behavior of the Japanese.

[8]
Japan's Built-In Cultural Obsession with Quality

THERE ARE A number of elements in Japan's culture that are unique to the Japanese—elements that make them different from other people, including Koreans and Chinese, their racial and cultural relatives.

This fundamental difference in the character of the Japanese can be attributed to the role that *Shintō* [Sheen-tohh], "The Way of the Gods," played in their lives until recent times.

Shintō is, in fact, a very sophisticated philosophy that incorporates the worship of nature in the tangible world and spirits in the invisible world—a phenomenon that has been common to mankind all over the world—but no other such nature-oriented society survived into modern times on the scale of the Japanese.

Japan's *Shintō*-based culture developed and survived for so long because the country was isolated from all other influences expect for nearby Korea and China—and in the process of absorbing these cultural influences form their neighbors the Japanese *Japanized* them.

But the influence that China [generally via Korea] had on Japan was significant and across the board, including the arts and crafts and it was this area that gave birth to the Japanese obsession with quality.

The Japanese formalized and institutionalized the Chinese and Korean apprenticeship practice in all of the arts and crafts. Apprenticeship started early, generally under the age of ten, and lasted for twenty to forty or more years.

The apprenticeships of those who succeeded their masters generally lasted for more than thirty years, as it was common for men to retire from formal positions at around forty-two years of age.

As each generation passed, the standards of quality in the arts and crafts edged upward, and well before the end of the remarkable Heian era [793-1185 A.D.] the work of the masters and their star apprentices had achieved the level of fine arts.

To artists, craftsmen and the public in general it became natural for them to expect the highest possible quality in the products they made and purchased. This level of quality was referred to as *atarimae hinshitsu* (ah-tah-ree-my heen-shee-tsuu) or "quality that is to be expected; that is normal; that is natural."

Today's younger Japanese are no longer overtly programmed in the *atarimae hinshitsu* mindset, but they naturally absorb a great deal of it as they grow up. Learning how to draw the complicated 1800-plus ideograms used to write their language plays a vital role in this programming.

Older Japanese, especially those born well before the turn of the century, still automatically expect a level of quality in the products they make and buy that can be disconcerting to Westerners—particularly to Americans who have been steeped in the "just good enough to get" by approach to quality.

In the 1970s and 80s I saw whole batches of American-made shirts, blouses and other wearing apparel turned down by Japanese wholesale buyers because the labels had the ends of threads sticking out.

When American importers first began to flock to Japan [way back in the 1890s!] to get goods copied cheap, the Japanese referred to these items as *Yokohama Hin* [Yokohama Heen] or "Yokohama Things"—meaning low-quality products to be shipped out of the country from Yokohama that they themselves would not buy.

This piece of American-Japanese history was repeated soon after the end of the Pacific War in 1945, but that time the Japanese were smarter. By the mid-1950s they had begun establishing their own importing and wholesaling operations in the U.S. and by the mid-1960s had dramatically increased the quality of the goods they made for export. The rest, as the saying goes, is history.

Foreigners wanting to sell products [and services] in Japan should learn and use the *atarimae hinshitsu* phraseology in their initial presentations and in their sales approaches. This will alert the Japanese that you understand their concern for quality and that you are also quality conscious on the *atarimae hinshitsu* level.

If you are not there yet, tell them that *atarimae hinshitsu* is the quality you intend to achieve, with their help.

[9]
The Importance of Dealing with Japan's Dynamic Diligence Factor!

IN 1953 AS a fledgling trade journalist in Tokyo I went to the dean of foreign correspondents in Japan [the Far Eastern Bureau Chief for a major London newspaper] and asked him if he thought it would be a good idea for me to stay in Japan—if there would be opportunities for me to build a worthwhile career, or if I should go home.

His instant response was: "Japan is never going to amount to anything! Go home!"

Just ten years later Japan was already on the verge of becoming the second largest economy in the world…and fortunately, I had not taken the famous correspondent's advice.

There are several reasons why Japan was able to recover so rapidly from the destruction of World War II. Two of these reasons are especially outstanding. First was the hundreds of millions of dollars pumped into the Japanese economy by the Allied Forces during the Occupation of the country from September 1945 to the spring of 1952. And second was the fact that the United States bought hundreds of millions of dollars worth of supplies from Japan during the Korean War [1950-1953].

An obvious third factor in why Japan was able to become an economic superpower by 1970 was the fact that from 1948 on Japanese manufacturers [that had spouted up like weeds following the end of WW II] were inundated by American importers who began flocking into the country by the thousands seeking consumer goods of all kinds at cheaper prices, giving this mass of new Japanese companies total access to the American market. [By the mid-1950s Sears had 65 buyers permanently stationed in Tokyo alone.]

This was not a sudden post-World War II phenomenon. The Japanese gained a world-wide reputation as a producer of cheap Western products within a decade after the Tokugawa Shogunate and samurai period officially ended in 1870, and the country was industrialized virtually overnight.

But undergirding all of the effort that went into the creation of the world's most efficient export industry, both in the late 1800s and following the end World War II in 1945, were a litany of national characteristics that made the Japanese both unique and formidable competitors.

One of the most important of these deeply ingrained cultural characteristics is subsumed in the word *monozukuri* (moe-no-zoo-kuu-ree)...a word that is so new it does not appear in most [if any!] dictionaries of Japanese words.

The applied meaning of *monozukuri* evolved from the meanings of its parts, including original thinking, the application of extraordinary efforts to achieve goals, craftsmanship, and diligence—all of which have traditionally been readily discernable in the character of the Japanese.

While all of these traits have made vital contributions to the economic success of the Japanese the one that is the most visible—at least to foreigners—is their built-in diligence.

For me, this remarkable trait was underscored in the 1970s when I was at a New York hotel for a business meeting that included a number of Japanese managers. I came down to the hotel restaurant before 6 a.m. for an early breakfast and found myself standing in line behind the Japanese.

I commented in Japanese to the man next to me that he and his co-workers were starting the day early. He replied with great emphasis and without smiling: *Kimben na Nihonjin desu kara!* ["Because we are diligent Japanese!"] The fact that the restaurant was already full of Americans did not appear to impress him.

The level of diligence in Japan is far higher than in most countries, and it expresses itself in everything they do...from the finish and the packaging of the products they make to the meticulous attention they pay to forging and maintaining their business contacts.

Many of the failures of American companies and U.S.-made products in Japan have been because they did not live up to the diligence standards of the Japanese. *Monozukuri* is a concept that must be taken to heart by any company wanting to succeed in the Japanese market.

[10]
The Japanese Secret
Of Mastering Anything!

ONE DAY when I was a resident of Tokyo and spent most Sunday mornings bowling with journalist friends I had a new kind of experience that was to have a profound influence on my understanding of how the Japanese go about achieving extraordinary skill in their pursuits.

I was serious about honing my bowling skill and was always fully conscious of every aspect of the physical movements involved in moving down the lane runway for two or three steps and releasing the ball.

But on this particular April morning I had been in a contemplative mood since getting up, and the mood continued while I walked the few blocks to the bowling alley in Meiji Park. The cherry blossoms were in full bloom, there was a mild breeze and the sky was a seductive blue. My mind virtually disassociated itself from my body and I was not conscious of the act of walking.

When I joined my friends at the bowling alley there was none of the usual banter and my mind remained more or less outside of my body. I was the first one up. I made my approach and let the ball go without thinking about it, and made a strike.

This body-mind disconnect continued and I got three more strikes in a row, at which point the thought suddenly occurred to me: "This is fantastic! I'm in a state of *muga* (muu-gah)!"

I became intensely conscious of what I was doing, and on my next time up my ball went into the gutter. I was beside myself with disgust at having broken the spell of *muga*.

The dictionary meaning of the Japanese word *muga* is self-effacement, a spiritual state of selflessness…to be in a state of ecstasy. But thanks to Japan's famous samurai class the term had come to mean much more than this esoteric definition.

From the age or six or seven boys in the samurai class went through a rigorous training process to develop incredible skill with the sword, and while they were mastering the physical process of wielding a sword they were also developing the ability to enter the mental state of *muga*—a state in which the mind did not interfere with the actions of their trained bodies.

The samurai were not the only Japanese to make use of the element of *muga* to achieve mastery in their profession. The training of all Japanese artists and craftsmen traditionally began in childhood and continued until they were in their thirties or forties and sometimes until they were in their fifties.

In this long process of mastering every physical element of their art or craft they also gradually got to the point that they did not have to think about the movements that were required to create a masterpiece. Their actions were spontaneous.

All people everywhere, especially those engaged in arts, crafts and other skills demanding precise, coordinated physical movements—from jugglers and musicians to sportspeople—must achieve some degree of *muga* in their actions to reach an impressive level of skill. But only those who are able to perform automatically on the highest level without thinking about the movements involved become true masters.

Not surprisingly, many of Japan's most famous Industrial entrepreneurs of the past have been *muga* devotees, pursuing this goal through Zen meditation.

It helps to have a word that explains the relationship between the body and the mind in developing a physical skill, and I recommend that the term *muga* be adopted by all cultures.

If young people are able to relate a long period of physical training with achieving the *muga* mind-state—during which performing a physical function perfectly becomes spontaneous—they might take their training more seriously.

Foreigners who have professional relationships with the Japanese will find knowledge of the *muga* concept an asset in all of their dealings with them. Among other things it helps explain their virtual obsession with details, structure, and precision in all of their efforts.

[11]
How the Japanese Build Success Into their Products

THE JAPANESE have traditionally been conditioned by their culture to achieve a profound degree of refinement in the products they build and to expect the same quality in the things they buy—a factor that must be taken into consideration in any effort to sell consumer products in Japan.

When Westerners first began to visit Japan in the mid-1540s they were struck by the refined beauty of the country's arts and crafts, which reflected a kind of beauty and utility that they had never seen before.

There was a character about Japanese-made things that gave them a look that was distinctive from similar things made in Korea and China, from which the original technology had come.

This special quality of Japanese things was so commonplace that the Japanese themselves did not consider it unusual. Everything they made, including ordinary household utensils, had the same quality.

After generations of refining their designs and techniques, Japan's master artists and craftsmen achieved a kind and quality of beauty that transcended the surface manifestations of their materials—a kind of beauty that is described as *yugen* (yuu-gane), meaning "mystery" or "subtlety."

Yugen beauty in Japanese products refers to a type of attractiveness—beneath the surface of the material but in delicate harmony with it—that registers on the conscious as well as the subconscious of the viewer, radiating a kind of spiritual essence.

By the 14th century the *yugen* qualities of Japan's arts and crafts had become so deeply embedded in the culture that they were not distinguished from daily life, and were reflected in everything the Japanese did, from their homes, interior decorations and gardens, to hand-made paper.

The distinctive arts and crafts of Japan owed their special character to a merging of cosmic and Shinto concepts of harmony, sensuality and spirituality—a cultural factor that remains very much in evidence among present-day Japanese artists and craftsmen…and in the mindset of most consumers.

The Shintō concept of harmony in Japanese products includes the size and shape of things, how they are to be used, and their relationship with people. The spiritual element in Japanese things is based on respecting the essence of the materials used and taking full advantage of their inherent qualities.

The sensual element in Japanese arts and crafts is reflected by the things that most people automatically find attractive—harmony in shape, in size, in the relationship of the parts, in the interaction of colors, in their feel when touched, and in the vibrations that emanate from them.

Despite the mostly Western façade that today's Japan presents to the world *yugen* beauty is still very much in evidence in the arts and crafts, in traditional restaurants, inns, shops, traditional wearing apparel and elsewhere in many unexpected places.

Yugen is another Japanese word I recommend that other people learn and use because it clearly identifies a concept that in other cultures requires several sentences to explain—and in itself is an example of the traditional Japanese propensity to refine things down to their essence.

The compulsive nature of the Japanese to refine consumer products is dramatically demonstrated in their ability to design and manufacture miniaturized hi-tech products and in using nanotechnology to create new processes and new materials.

Achieving the *yugen* character and quality of products is one of the cultural barriers foreign manufacturers of consumer goods generally have to overcome before they can succeed in Japan…and is the reason why some French-made products often outsell their American-made counterparts in Japan.

For a more definitive discussion of the Japanese view and creation of *yugen* beauty see my book: *ELEMENTS OF JAPANESE DESIGN—Key Terms for Understanding & Using Japan's Classic Wabi-Sabi-Shibui Concept.* [Tuttle Publishing].

[12]
How the Japanese Tap
Into Cosmic Creativity!

UNTIL RECENT TIMES the Western world did not give very much thought to the relationship between the mind and the body, and to the power of the mind to influence and change the functioning of the body. Such ideas were regarded as mystic nonsense.

It was not until the latter part of the 1900s that Western scientists began to accept the idea that their concepts of the physical world were only a part of the human and cosmic equation, and that there was much more to life and existence than what meets the eye.

Most people in the West continue to ignore the ancient Asian practice of Zen, which allows one to transcend conventional wisdom, see things as they really are, and achieve mental and physical skills that are out of the ordinary.

It was the addition of Zen meditation to the training of Japan's famous samurai class that made it possible for them to transcend the limitations of the average person in martial arts, and it was this same training that provided the insight for Japan's artists, craftsmen and garden designers to routinely create masterpieces.

One of the versions of Zen that has played a key role in the emergence of Japan as a major economic power is subsumed in the word *jizai* (jee-zie), which, in effect, refers to being able to think outside of the box of conventional wisdom and customary practices.

Virtually all of Japan's best known businessmen /entrepreneurs have been and still are practitioners of *jizai,* and the concept is the foundation of many of the think-tanks that sprung up in Japan in the latter half of the 20th century—the best known of which is the *Jizai Kenkyu Jo* (Jee-zie Kane-que Jo), or Jizai Research Institute, founded in 1970 by Masahiro Mori, a Tokyo University professor of engineering who was also the founder of the Robotics Society of Japan.

Many of the most successful products that Japan has produced since that time have been the result of *jizai* thinking. In product terms, *jizai* thinking means meditating on the design and function of a product until you arrive at the ultimate in function, design and quality.

There was very little if any tradition of this kind in the Western world until recent times, particularly in the United States, and it was not until competition from Japanese manufacturers became a serious threat to U.S. industry that some American designers and engineers began to take a more *jizai* approach to their work.

Still today, however, most Westerners, especially typical American businesspeople, bureaucrats and politicians, view themselves and the rest of the world in two dimensions at most. This accounts for most of the ill-conceived and badly implemented policies that are endemic in the economy, education, government on all levels, and society in general.

This cultural failing is not likely to be overcome until *jizai*-type thinking becomes an integral part of the world's cultures. For one thing, *jizai*-thinking is not based on the concept that profit comes first. It is based on the idea that if you design and build the best possible product, people will be attracted to it and buy it.

[13]
The Extraordinary Role of the Kawaii [Kah-wah-eee] or "Cute" Syndrome in Japanese Culture

ONE OF THE things that foreign retailers wanting to do business in Japan should know about is the importance of the "cute" factor in everyday Japanese life.

To my knowledge, most men in the world grow out of the attachment to cute things and cute behavior that is typical of babies and toddlers, and is especially exemplified by girls when they are young and by most women of whatever age.

In Japan, however, there has traditionally been a powerful feminine element in Japanese culture that applied to both males and females, including tough male samurai warriors.

My reading of this element is that it evolved from the extraordinary sophistication of the Japanese in their appreciation of natural and manmade beauty, the extraordinary refinement of their traditional etiquette, and the refinement and sophistication of their arts, crafts and formal wearing apparel—the latter restricting the movement of both males and females to what has traditionally been equated with feminine behavior.

Until the latter part of the 1950s Japanese girls in particular were programmed to behave in an infantile cute manner from the age of babyhood and to continue this behavior as young adults—something that has great seductive appeal to males.

One of the most common ploys used by young women working in cabarets and clubs as hostesses to attract males and separate them from big tips was to put on a baby act.

This cute factor was not—and still today is not—limited to the world of cabarets and clubs. It is a major factor in the design of products and in print advertising across the board and in television commercials.

Many Japanese companies specialize in selling *kawaii* [kah-wah-eee] or "cute" things. One of the most successful of Japan's *kawaii* sellers is Sanrio Company, the creator in 1974 of Hello Kitty, a cute cat that soon morphed into a trade name that gave birth to an international conglomerate on the order of Disney characters and products that brings in millions of dollars annually.

At the turn of the century Sanrio had only ten Hello Kitty products in its lineup. By 2009 that number had jumped to seventy and covered a variety of wares, from dolls, ceramics, lacquerware and rice bowls to high-end chopsticks—the latter priced at some $60.00!

A growing number of foreign companies have taken a page out of Japan's *kawaii* book and learned how to get on the cute bandwagon, not only in products aimed at children and girls but in adult "toys" like automobiles and motorcycles, laptop computers and toilet ware.

Foreign businesspeople interested in getting into the Japanese market—or increasing their sales in their own home markets—should include a course in *kawaii* as part of their planning—something the Japanese don't have to be concerned about because they do it automatically.

The secret of *kawaii* appeal is a combination of miniaturization, extraordinary refinement down to the smallest detail, no abrupt angles, the use of oval-shapes because oval shapes are sensually seductive [while squares and rectangles are not], and very large eyes in dolls and in the depiction of animals and humans.

When put together, these factors work like magic on both a conscious and subconscious level.

[14]
Japan's Communications and Cultural "Black Hole!"

DURING THE 1950s and early 1960s I often described Japan as being a "black hole" when it came to information relating to corporate Japan and the government.

Like "black holes" in the galaxies, companies and government agencies sucked in information from around the world but never gave anything back. Companies and government agencies collected tons of domestic data, but it was not made available to the public, in part because of cultural reasons.

The barriers to obtaining business information about Japan were not fully breached until the proliferation of computers in the 1980s and the accompanying seismic shift in the mindset of the Japanese.

But Japan now suffers from a "communications **and** cultural black hole" that impacts on domestic matters and as well as its international relationships. The reasons for this problem are also both linguistic and cultural.

A Tokyo University professor has noted that the Japanese language is so obtuse, so inexact, that often only about 70 percent of one hears the first time is clear, requiring further explanation that often is not forthcoming.

On the international front the main reason for Japan's communications "black hole" is the fact that so few Japanese on that level are bilingual or bicultural, and they continue to have a built-in Japan-is-unique bias.

From the late 1630s until the 1860s Japan was virtually closed to the outside world, and regarded its language as one of the most important barriers in keeping foreigners at bay.

Near the end of this period of isolation, when foreigners began pounding on Japan's doors, the shogunate government passed an edict making it a capital crime to teach Japanese to foreigners. Furthermore, any Japanese who learned a foreign language was regarded as a traitor or potential traitor, and was kept under surveillance.

As late as the 1960s most Japanese automatically assumed that Westerners could not learn Japanese, and were dumbfounded when they encountered one who did. At the same time, the Japanese approach to encouraging and requiring the study of English for business and political purposes was even more myopic than the traditional American approach to the study of foreign languages.

Mandatory English lessons in Japanese schools were taught by Japanese teachers who could read English but could not speak it or understand it when spoken.

By the 1970s, however, this situation had improved significantly, with hundreds of public and private schools employing foreign language teachers and many companies hiring foreign tutors to teach English in-house to key employees.

There has since been a very conspicuous increase in the number of Japanese [especially girls and women] who can speak and understand English well.

But on the business and political front the number of Japanese who speak English—the main language of international business and diplomacy—is still so small Japan's news media warns that the country is on the verge of being left behind the rest of the world.

The problem—which the United States has also faced and not yet fully recognized—is that the Japanese were conditioned over the centuries to look inward instead of outward, to have a built-in isolationist "Japan is different" complex.

The fact that Japan was able to become an extremely rich nation in just 25 years [thanks to the American and European markets] while still limiting its involvement with the outside world has allowed most Japanese to maintain their isolationist mindset.

Language remains a primary cultural barrier not only for the Japanese but for Americans as well. As noted in an earlier column universal language translators [which will be readily available by 2015] will reduce this problem but will not solve it.

Languages do not automatically convey their cultural content, so language-learning [and the use of translation devices] must be combined with cultural learning, and this is an area that has gotten little attention in many countries, if not ignored altogether, especially by Japan and the United States.

Both Japan and the United States have increased their number of foreign language-cultural programs, but they are far behind China, India and most other countries—and this puts Japanese and Americans at a serious economic and political disadvantage.

[15]
The Kiryaku Element
In the Character of the Japanese

As is often the case in Japan's Japanized yin-yang culture, many of the cultural elements have both positive and negative sides—and while the Japanese are acutely aware of these contradictory factors they often must accept and deal with them because they have no choice.

One of the most important of the plus elements in Japanese culture is subsumed in the two words *kiryaku juō* (kee-r'yah-kuu juu-ohh), which means something like "being resourceful across the board"—that is, capable of reacting efficiently and effectively to changing circumstances of whatever kind.

The underlying implication of this concept is that in order to be fully resourceful you must be aware of everything that is going on in your in your area of interest and in your market—a factor that accounts for the obsessive and insatiable appetite the Japanese have for both domestic and international information.

This means, of course, that the Japanese take the time and spend the resources to study and dissect things to an extent that is typically well beyond what is common among Americans and other nationalities—a factor that often gives them an advantage in devising their manufacturing and marketing strategies.

It has been said that the worldwide intelligence networks of Japan's famous trading companies [Mitsui, Mitsubishi, etc.] are more extensive and more successful in garnering valuable information than the intelligence arms of most major governments.

[16]
Understanding and Experiencing The Japanese Concept of Mono no Aware [Moe-no no Ah-wah-ray]

THE JAPANESE have long had a reputation abroad as being "economic animals" who give work precedence over having a good time—and to some extent they deserve this reputation. Each year a number of Japanese commit *karoshi* (kah-roe-she). In other words they work themselves to death!

But there is another side of Japan that is wonderfully uplifting—and here is my personal take on that side.

One of the special elements of Japanese culture is the tradition of creating both environments and occasions for communing with the fragility of life—an element that adds enormously to the recognition of this fragility and makes people more inclined to enjoy the years they have.

One of the most memorable afternoons I have spent in Japan was in a traditional *ryokan* (rio-kahn), inn, situated on the slope of a gorge on picturesque Izu Peninsula southwest of Tokyo. It was a Sunday afternoon. I was alone, and it was raining—not a heavy rain but a light, steady rain that was close to being a mist. I was sitting on the balcony of my room, looking out over the gorge, waiting for a friend to arrive.

As I sat there staring contemplatively at this incredibly beautiful sight I began to experience what the Japanese call *mono no aware* (moe-no no ah-wah-ray)—a Buddhist concept that includes being very conscious of the ephemeral nature of man, his struggle in the face of great odds and the inevitability of his downfall and disappearance.

This aspect of Japan's culture, developed between 700 and 1200 A.D. was based on the acute recognition of the impermanence of all things—an element that was enhanced by the code of the samurai which required them to be ready to give up their lives at a moment's notice— resulting in their lives being compared to cherry blossoms...beautiful but fragile to the extreme and subject to being wafted away by the slightest breeze.

This culture of impermanence was especially reflected in the haiku and tanka poetry of the era, as well as in the such great literary works as *Genji Monogatari* (The Tale of Genji), a novel about the intrigues and loves of an imperial prince (usually regarded as the world's first novel) written in the early 11th century by Murasaki Shikibu, a lady in the Imperial Court in Kyoto; and *Heike Monogatari* (The Tale of the Heike), compiled by a blind monk named Kakuichi in 1371.

The opening lines of *Heike Monogatari*, which depicts an epic struggle between the Taira and Minamoto clans for the control of Japan in the 12th century, say more about the human condition than many philosophical tomes:

"The sound of the Gion Shôja [temple bells in the Gion district of Kyoto] echoes the impermanence of all things; the color of the sâla flowers reveals the truth that the prosperous must decline. The proud do not endure; they are like a dream on a spring night. The mighty fall at last; they are as dust before the wind."

The culture of Japan reflected this theme in many ways, resulting in the Japanese developing an extensive vocabulary that expressed this inherent sadness of life.

While *mono no aware* means something like "indulging one's self in grief," neither this phrase nor any of the other key words were actually used in sad situations. Instead they referred to a gentle melancholy view of the fragility and preciousness of life that included an element of subdued pleasure

The annual custom of celebrating the short life of cherry blossoms is the largest and most popular of Japan's *mono no aware* rituals. It reminds them to take the time and find ways to enjoy life while they can because it will soon be gone.

My spending a quiet afternoon entranced by the natural beauty of the setting as it was being cleansed and renewed by rain was another of the *mono no aware* practices that are dear to the hearts of the Japanese. Still another way is to engage in "forest bathing"—spending time in an isolated forest, letting the sights, sounds and vibrations of the trees wash over you.

There is also an element of *mono no aware* in most of Japan's classic art and craft designs, from kitchen utensils to the kimono wore by older men and women. The famous Tea Ceremony is a pure *mono no aware* ritual.

Knowledge of this cultural element makes it possible for one to appreciate more fully the distinctive essence of things Japanese—the elements that make them Japanese.

This factor is one of the unspoken and generally un-described things that make the traditional aspects of life in Japan so sensually, intellectually and spiritually attractive to everyone, including foreigners who are sensitive to the realities of the brevity of life.

KOREA

[1]

The Role of "The Force" in South Korea

AS THE WORLD knows, South Korea is a tiny nation on the southern half of the Korean Peninsula that in thirty remarkable years transformed itself from a war-torn basket-case into one of the larger economies in the world, with huge industrial conglomerates that sell their high-tech products worldwide.

However, *how* this tiny nation was able to transform itself into an economic powerhouse in less than one generation is not well known—and today relates in an alarming way to changes that have occurred in the United States in the last half a century.

There are two primary things that help explain the amazing success of South Korea following the end of the Korean War [1950-1953]—a debacle caused by Washington politicians agreeing to allow the Soviet Union to occupy the northern half of the peninsula at the end of World War II, which led to the Communist regime that has since kept the country in lock-down.

Despite the fact that the U.S. withdrew most of its troops from South Korea soon after the end of World War II—which invited the North Korean invasion in 1950—the U.S. did manage to sponsor an incipient kind of democracy in South Korea that grew slowly, eventually making it possible for capitalism and a consumer economy to flourish.

The second factor that played a fundamental role in the incredible rise of South Korea is subsumed in the word *han* (hahn), which Korean scholars translate as "unrequited resentments"—which has to be explained because it means so much more than that phrase suggests.

My own definition is that *han* refers to all of the natural physical and emotional impulses, all of the ambitions and desires, all of the creative impulses and spirit of the Koreans that were oppressed and denied by the previous governments from the 15th century until recent times.

When all of these repressed feelings were released by South Koreans being freed from the oppression and restraints of the past, the energy, power and passion they were able to bring to their efforts to create a modern, rich economy must have been seen to be fully appreciated.

This pent-up energy and passion of South Koreans has not yet expended itself, and going there and seeing the ferocity, dedication and diligence with which the people continue to work today is a mind-blowing experience, especially for Americans.

Americans, on the other hand, have lost much of the "*han*" power that made the United States unique among nations. The first Americans were energized and enthused by something similar to the *han* of Korea, because they too had been oppressed and suppressed by the religious, economic and political systems of Europe, and came to the New World to escape them.

But the American version of *han* has dissipated dramatically in the last several decades and no longer makes up the core of the Establishment culture. We have become a society that is over-fed, over-drugged, over-indulged, under-educated, under-challenged, and ignores reality.

While the United States, Japan and South Korea are incredible examples of what can happen when people who are hungry and ambitious are allowed to help themselves, this is only a minor prelude to what is happening in China, and what this portends for the future of the world.

When Xiaoping Deng became the paramount leader of China in 1978 and shortly thereafter announced that "to get rich is glorious," it formally released the one billion-plus Chinese from the *han* chains that had bound them for millennia.

Given the history of China, the power of the *han* of the Chinese may very well be greater than the *han* of the rest of Asia combined. The image and role that has been in the psyche of educated Chinese for millennia has been that of the supreme power and the benevolent ruler of the world at large.

[2]
The Indomitable Spirit of Koreans

LIKE SO MANY of our prejudiced views of the people of the world one of the post-WWII images of Korea was originally associated with a single word. In this case, "Gook," a corruption of the Korean word *Hanguk* (Hahn-guuk), which means "Korean Nation."

Somehow, during the Korean War [1950-1953] American GI's shortened *Hanguk* into "Gook," first as an easy-to-remember and pronounce epithet for Koreans, and finally as a derogatory term that came to be used to express a growing dislike and contempt for Koreans.

The derogatory use of the term "Gook" quickly made its way to the American Occupation forces still in Japan, where it was indiscriminately applied to the Japanese and Chinese as well—and for the next two or three decades helped to create a false and misleading image of Koreans, Japanese and Chinese among many Americans...and image that contributed to them being underestimated by American business as well as government leaders.

The point of this odd introduction to the term *Hanguk* is to once again emphasize how powerful a single word can be in the mindset and behavior of a people. To Koreans *Hanguk* is a semi-sacred phrase that incorporates their incredibly powerful feelings for their country and their national identity.

The last line in the Korean national anthem, *Ae Guk Ga* (Aye Guuk Gah), literally "Love Country Song" [written in 1896], does more to explain the pride and passion that North and South Koreans have in their nations than anything else I can think of. It goes like this: "Let us love, come grief, come gladness, this, our beloved land!"

But to fully appreciate the passion and pride that all Koreans have traditionally had in their land you have to be a Korean—you have to know its history; its glories, its tragedies...especially its tragedies.

Over the past two and a half millennia the Korean Peninsula has been invaded and occupied by the Chinese, the Mongols and the Japanese, and when they were not fighting outsiders they were savaged by internal regional conflicts—and yet, despite these travails, Korean culture produced some of the world's greatest works of art, created masterpieces of poetry and made technical advances (including movable type for printing!) far earlier than any other people.

Another reason for the pride Koreans take in their nation is the natural beauty of the peninsula. The native religion of the Koreans, like that of the Japanese Ainu and American Indians, included the belief that they were a part of nature, and that recognizing and respecting the beauty of nature was a key part of their being.

In the 1990s the government of South Korea passed some of the most farsighted legislation in the world to expand and protect its forests and parks and the ambiance of its cities by making large set-backs and greenery mandatory for new buildings.

Knowing the way Koreans feel about their country and fully respecting their feelings, can be a major asset for foreigners visiting and living in Korea. Much of this benefit comes from indicating knowledge and interest in Korean culture.

Establishing good, cooperative relationships with Koreans, and sustaining them, begins and ends with understanding and reacting effectively to the way they think and behave.

One of the first cultural elements in the character of Koreans that is essential for foreigners to learn and deal with is that individually they are not passive and reticent like the Japanese, or group-dependent like the Japanese. They are independent and volatile, and do not back down in a dispute or back away from a fight.

[3]
Beware of the Korean Shame Syndrome

ONE OF THE elements of the Korean mindset that often poses a special problem and danger for Westerners is the role of *changpi* (chahng-pee), or shame, in the culture—a role that is so deeply ingrained in Korean attitudes and behavior that it is one of the primary foundations of their national character.

Instead of being programmed by a religion to feel guilt as a result of wrong doing, and being subject to punishment by the creators and keepers of this method of social control, Koreans have traditionally been conditioned to feel intense shame when they are guilty of or are accused of wrong-doing, as well as when someone fails to follow the institutionalized rules of etiquette and morality in their relationships with them, thereby damaging their "face."

As it happens, this system turns out to be a more powerful control mechanism than religious-based guilt feelings, resulting in Koreans in general being far better behaved than their religious-guilt oriented counterparts in other countries.

The role of shame in Korean culture derives from the influence of Confucianism, which teaches that personal shame should be the basis of all morality—not religious concepts that promise punishment in an afterlife or secular laws that call for punishment in real life.

In religious-based guilt cultures, especially Christianized cultures, people who are guilty of wrongdoing may suffer from guilt feelings but their suffering is generally not visible and does not necessarily affect the behavior of others toward them.

In such societies people can do the most horrendous things and if they are not somehow caught they can behave as if they are innocent and live normal lives, well-treated by family, friends and others. Many, in fact, take false pride in having gotten away with something.

In Korea, on the other hand, cultural conditioning in the Confucian concept of *changpi* results in Koreans who commit visible etiquette infractions or secular crimes against others punishing themselves by intense feelings of shame whether they are exposed or not.

Conversely, when someone fails to behave in the prescribed and ritualized manner toward Koreans they regard it as a major transgression against them—as an insult that must be avenged in order for them to maintain their "face."

Traditionally, the sense of shame instilled in Koreans was collective. It went beyond individuals to include their families, their clan, their region of the country and ultimately the whole country. In other words, if you insulted one Korean you insulted all Koreans.

In earlier times, one of the major sources of shame for male Koreans was failing to live up to the expectations of their families—their fathers and grandfathers, their close kin and their clan. This shame factor was one of the primary sources of the drive of Koreans to get the best possible education and the extraordinary diligence the vast majority display in their work.

Koreans still live in a shame-controlled culture—which is weaker than what it used to be but by Western standards is still incredibly strong. It is therefore important for foreigners dealing with Koreans to know enough about the culture to be aware of the kind of things that result in shame—and both avoid them and learn how to deal with them if they happen inadvertently.

There are a whole litany of things that Koreans regard as shaming, beginning with failure to abide by the rules of etiquette and morality that cover all relationships, including those pertaining to sexual gender, age, educational level, job-rank, and social class. [See *Etiquette Guide to Korea* and *Korean Business Etiquette*.]

North Korea is, of course, a special case. On a government level, the traditional shame-based morality and etiquette have been over-laid by a paranoid communist ideology that is irrational and inhuman, making it virtually impossible to have a rational, equitable, constructive relationship with North Korean officialdom.

[4]
The Importance of "Face" In Korea

BECAUSE OF THE importance of social class, rank, and precise behavioral forms in pre-modern Korea all Koreans became incredibly sensitive about the behavior of others as well as their own behavior because there were so many ways they could get into trouble.

Doing something that made someone else "lose face" or yourself losing face was not a trivial thing. It could be, and often was, disastrous—and it is still something that cannot be taken lightly.

This cultural factor gave birth to *chae-myun* (chay-me-yuun) or "face-saving" as one of the most important—and demanding—aspects of Korean life.

As noted in *Korea's Business & Cultural Code Words*, speaking clearly and candidly is one of the things that was traditionally taboo in Korea. Speech became indirect and vague. Direct criticism, especially of superiors, was prohibited and there were serious consequences for breaking the ban.

These rules of behavior, implemented following the beginning of the Choson dynasty in1392, were so detailed and encompassing that they had a fundamental impact on the Korean language itself, which then became a primary means of passing this cult-like behavior on to succeeding generations.

This remarkable development, which evolved from the formal and official adoption of a much sterner version of Confucianism combined with the already hierarchical segregation of social classes, resulted in Korean cultural becoming locked in a time-warp with virtually no change until the latter decades of the 19th century—a 400-plus year period during which the country was known to the outside world as "The Hermit Kingdom."

Korea's Hermit Kingdom era did not come to an end until the late 1800s when the Japanese, Russians, Americans and other foreigners arrived and began carving the country up into areas of interest.

The Japanese were the most aggressive, defeating Russia in the 1904-1905 war and soon thereafter invading Korea, annexing the country in1910 and turning it into a colony. But during the Japanese period, which lasted until 1945, the traditional elements of Korean culture were virtually unchanged.

Still today *chae-myum* continues to be a major factor in all relationships in Korea, particularly in work environments and in all professional categories—with gender, age, education and other not so obvious factors involved.

The way Koreans go about saving and repairing face often does not conform to Western concepts of what is necessary, right or acceptable—a situation that often causes friction between foreigners and Koreans working in the same company.

In fact, some of the solutions Koreans choose are so far out from what would be a Western approach that they result in an impasse if not a complete breakdown in relationships.

The traditional Korean methods for avoiding and dealing with loss of face include withholding bad news [especially if it happens on a Friday], not telling the truth, and resorting to an old institutionalized practice of repairing the damage by mutually agreeing to pretend that it never happened.

When a loss of face occurs among Korean employees of foreign companies the situation can be serious, whether it involves only the Korean side or the foreign side as well.

Among the problems that occur in foreign companies: promoting a younger person over older people; promoting a graduate of a less prestigious school over employees of the same age who graduated from a brand university; showing favoritism to an employee...and especially showing favoritism toward an employee who speaks English.

It is therefore important for foreign managers in Korea to establish and maintain close relationships with as many of their employees as possible so they will be more likely to learn about serious "face" problems and have an opportunity to work out mutually agreeable solutions.

[5]
The Importance of "Peace of Mind" In Korean Relationships

IT MAY BE a bit difficult to accept the idea that Koreans have a deeply embedded need and desire for *anshim* (ahn-sheem), or "peace of mind," after you have engaged in a bargaining session or had a personal encounter with a Korean.

Koreans regularly engaged in loud arguments and verbal fights that can be upsetting to those who don't know what is going on—and in this respect they have sometimes been referred to as "The Irish of the Orient!"

The propensity of Koreans to engage in both verbal and physical battles is also at odds with an ancient Chinese description of the Korean Peninsula as "The Land of Morning Calm."

Subsequent views of the calm nature of Koreans have traditionally been reflected in the arts, including portraits of elderly retired gentlemen sitting in perfect repose in their traditional attire.

But these views have been misleading. During the 15th century fighting among Korean men was so endemic that the king [Sejong] issued an edict requiring adult males to wear heavy hats made of clay, with the proviso that if they got into a fight that was serious enough for the hats to fall off of their heads they would be severely punished.

[I don't know how it could have happened but this ancient custom must have given rise to the old English saying of "fighting at the drop of a hat."]

Still, the role of *anshim* in Korean relationships is of vital importance, and can be traced to the influence of Buddhism and Confucianism, both of which had a powerful impact on the mindset of Koreans, programming them to be at ease and comfortable only in settings that were highly structured and all of the traditional forms of etiquette were followed precisely.

Obviously, however, this programming did not preclude loud verbal bouts and even physical action when they were done within the accepted guidelines of behavior.

In today's Korea the concept and importance of *anshim* continues to play a leading role. Korean culture continues to support the ideal of doing nothing to disturb the peace of mind of other people in the use of language, in personal behavior, in the ethics they follow in business, and so on.

The main thing for foreigners to keep in mind is that *anshim* in Korea does not mean the same thing as "peace of mind" does in the Western world. Some of the demands and dictates in Korea's business world, for example, go against everything Westerners hold dear.

Among other things, a Korean manager will publicly and loudly lambast an employee, or group of employees, in the strongest terms for some failure or mishap—something that is, however, a definite no-no for foreign managers in Korea.

Koreans distinguish between their own behavior and the behavior they will accept from foreigners, and these differences can be so subtle only a Korean, or a foreigner who is deeply steeped in Korean culture, picks up on them.

For most foreigners in Korea this means relying on trusted Korean employees to provide the insights and guidelines that are necessary to maintain *anshim* in business settings.

[6]
The Critical Role of Friendship Networks in Korea

FRIENDSHIPS ARE obviously important in all societies for business as well as social reasons, but few people go as far as Koreans in their need and compulsion to develop and keep a network of *chingu* (cheen-goo) or friends.

The reason for this extraordinary phenomenon is that traditionally Koreans could not depend upon anyone except people with whom they had close personal and family ties...basically for anything... often including services that local officials and bureaucrats were legally obliged to do for them.

The obligations that family members had to each other and to their family as a whole virtually precluded them from establishing close relationships with more than a few outsiders.

The reason for this extraordinary situation was that in Korean culture friendships entailed a number and a degree of obligations that went far beyond what was common in the Western world, and could have a seriously negative impact on the lives of both the individuals and their families.

Outside contacts were therefore severely limited. Most Korean women spent their lives without ever speaking to, much less spending time with, anyone not a member of their family or close kin.

For one long period in the more recent history of Korea women in urban areas could not leave their family compounds during the day to shop or pay social visits. They were allowed to leave their homes for a few hours only at night, during which men were required by law to stay indoors to prevent them from intermingling with women who were not members of their family.

Korean men had a lot more freedom than women, but their relationships outside of their families and childhood contacts were generally limited to a few men they met in bars and *kisaeng* (kee-sang) houses—Korean "geisha" houses.* They were not free to develop a circle of friends in the casual way that is common in Western countries because of the weight of the obligations that came with the friendships.

These social and political restrictions were officially abolished near the end of the 1800s [as a result of Western influence], but it was to be several decades before both men and women in Korea felt free to exercise the kind of personal freedoms Americans and others take for granted when it comes to friendships.

However, the legacy of the past continues to influence the behavior of Koreans when it comes to making and sustaining friends. Koreans, especially businesspeople and politicians, now go out of their way to develop and maintain a circle of friends because generally that they are able to get things done only through friends...a point that foreigners in Korea need to be aware of.

Cold calls are still rare in Korea, and getting cooperation and/or help from people you don't already have a close relationship is also rare.

It is strongly recommended that foreign businesspeople, diplomats and others who take up residence in Korea for any purpose quickly begin a planned campaign to develop and sustain friendships with people in official and professional positions as well as with their contemporaries in age, education and occupation who have their own networks of friends.

These relationships are made and sustained the same way they are in the U.S. and elsewhere—through frequent meetings in bars and restaurants, doing favors for each other, giving gifts to the individuals and to their wives and children on special occasions, participating in recreational activities with your peers, and so on.

By the 1970s Korean businesspeople had also adopted the American custom of breakfast meetings, business luncheons, and inviting their Korean as well as their foreign contacts to bars and nightclubs afterhours.

Nightclubs quickly became the most popular of these nighttime venues because they were staffed by some of the most beautiful and seductive women in the world...and like their Japanese counterparts Korean businesspeople were skilled at cementing both friendships and business deals in that stimulating atmosphere.*

*Koreans, not the Japanese, invented the institutionalized and ritualized profession of using beautiful women to help them develop and maintain business and political relationships. The kisaeng of Korea predated the geisha of Japan by about one thousand years. See below.

[7]
Beware of the Bargaining Skill of Koreans!

OVER THE DECADES I have observed a deep-seated tendency for American and other Western businesspeople on their first outings in Asia to be especially careful about inadvertently antagonizing or insulting their Asian counterparts by some kind of cultural slip-up.

Being sensitive to cultural differences is, of course, imperative in successfully establishing and sustaining business and political relationships with Asians and others!

But there is invariably a point and a time when being more sensitive than is expected or necessary becomes a major disadvantage to the Western side. When this happens—and it often does—the foreign side loses to some degree.

There is, perhaps, no better example of this syndrome than when Westerners are engaged in negotiating with Koreans...and when continuing to engage in relationships with Koreans after an agreement of whatever kind has been "reached."

There are two important factors that must be taken into consideration when dealing with Koreans. First, Koreans

have a powerful tradition of *enuri* (eh-nuu-ree) or bargaining. The nature of the traditional culture of Korea made it
absolutely essential that individuals become especially
skilled at bargaining in virtually every area of their lives.

Relationships between the sexes, between social classes
and in business and political situations were [and still are
to a considerable degree] strictly structured and enforced,
making it vital that individuals learn how to stretch the
limitations of their positions as far as possible by their verbal skills.

One aspect of this bargaining factor evolved from the
fact that until modern times in Korea the prices of goods
were not fixed. There were no widely established principles for setting the cost of goods or the value of labor. It
was a matter of choice and need.

Today [South] Korean department stores, fine boutiques,
restaurants and the like have fixed prices, but in the great
city markets, *enuri* (eh-nuu-ree) or haggling, to use a
colloquial term, is still practiced with gusto by merchants
and shoppers. If you don't haggle you will get the short
end of the stick.

Just important as the haggling skills of Koreans is the
fact that they are culturally conditioned to use emotion in
their bargaining and negotiations—and they are extremely
clever at using emotional tactics to get what they want.

This pertains to all relationships. If you want to see and
hear something startling to Western eyes and ears just be in
the near vicinity of a Korean woman when she believes she
had been wronged by a man or wants something from a
man!

Korean businesspeople, bureaucrats and politicians
typically use everything in their emotional arsenal when
dealing with foreigners—something that throws typical
Westerners [men in particular] for a loop because they

have little or no experience in using emotion as a bargaining tool and in getting their way after deals are signed.

Koreans typically turn the negotiation of simple points into high drama by introducing various kinds of emotional elements, which frequently includes shouting. When this happens, the thing to do is to remain calm and collected and stick to your guns until your Korean counterparts accept the idea that you are not going to be bamboozled into anything.

And whatever you do don't get on the wrong side of a Korean woman!

[8]
Bring on the Kisaeng
[and the Geisha]!

SINCE ANCIENT TIMES Chinese and Korean businessmen and government officials have used the sensual appeal and entertainment skills of young women as integral elements in creating and maintaining their professional relationships. [As noted above the Japanese were late comers to this practice.]

This custom appeared very early in China, apparently at least three thousand years ago, where it was centered on the Imperial Court and the highest echelons of government. Chinese courts maintained large numbers of women to serve and entertain higher officials and their guests—with "scouts" seeking out the most beautiful girls in Korea and other tributary states and shipping them to China.

Early in Korea's "Three Kingdoms Period" [roughly 57 B.C. to 669 A.D.] troupes of attractive young women trained in singing and dancing, known as *yorak* (yoh-rahk), or "entertainers," became permanent parts of the kings' courts and the various ministries of the three governments.

As time passed, these young women came to be known as *kisaeng* (kee-sang), or "art persons," and their numbers and influence increased dramatically. In addition to entertaining their patrons and the friends and guests of their patrons they were also dispatched to entertain troops who were stationed in remote areas.

The fortunes of the *kisaeng* waxed and waned over the centuries since they also served as mistresses and prostitutes and were often controversial, but they were to achieve their heyday during the Choson Dynasty, which began in 1392 and lasted until the end of the 19th century.

During this period they became the best-educated, best-dressed and most elite women in the country, and their training and upkeep evolved into a major part of the nation's commerce. [History records that in the 1870s over 10,000 of them were attached to the Imperial Court!]

The number and role of the *kisaeng* has diminished dramatically in modern Korea, but the institution continues to exist on a small scale and *kisaeng* houses are still patronized by businesspeople and government officials who also use them to entertain themselves and foreign guests.

In Japan, on the other hand, the institution of the *geisha*—the Japanese counterparts of the *kisaeng*—did not appear until the latter decades of the 17th century—first as entertainers for the most elite courtesans of the day, and it was not until the last decades of the 19th century that they replaced courtesans as the entertainers of choice by Japan's elite.

By the outbreak of the Pacific War in 1941 there were some 80,000 *geisha* in Japan, and they had become an integral part of Japan's business and political world—only to be mostly replaced by some 500,000 cabaret hostesses soon after the end of the war in 1945.

Now there are only an estimated 2,000 professional geisha in Japan [most of them in Kyoto], but in the meantime something quite remarkable has happened.

A combination of movies, books and television has romanticized the popular image of the geisha and now a growing number of ordinary Japanese girls are apprenticing themselves to geisha in Kyoto to gain the social skills they epitomize.

As is typical in Japan, sociologists and academics in various fields have joined in the public discourse about this phenomenon, virtually guaranteeing that it will continue to grow.

While small numbers of foreign businessmen and government dignitaries are taken to geisha inns by their Japanese hosts, large numbers are taken to cabarets and nightclubs that feature attractive hostesses.

Korean and Japanese hosts invite their foreign counterparts to *kisaeng* and *geisha* houses and to hostess-stocked nightclubs as a way of breaking down the cultural barriers between them. They know from long experience that interacting together with good-looking women is the fastest way to accomplish that goal.

In earlier times, the ultimate way for two Japanese men to achieve the closest possible relationship was to arrange to enjoy the favors of the same woman at the same setting—a custom, according to some, that has not completely disappeared.

***

No culture can live if it attempts
to be exclusive.

—Mahatma Gandhi—

***

MEXICO

IN MY BOOK *There's a Word for It in Mexico!* I note that all languages are reflections of the emotional, spiritual and intellectual character of the people who created them, and that the older, more structured and more exclusive a society and its language, the more terms it has that are pregnant with cultural nuances that control the attitudes and behavior of the people.

To begin with [again quoting myself], the character of Mexicans is made up of a blend of Indian, Moorish, and Spanish authoritarianism combined with medieval Catholicism, which produced a society steeped in religious rituals, personalism, machoism, a tendency for violence and —surprisingly perhaps—"an inherently sad-joyful nature that manifests in singing, dancing and art.

As a result of this extraordinary mixture of cultures and spiritual cults Mexico's traditional values and morals were forged in a caldron of aggressive religious intolerance, corruption, racism, male chauvinism, and an elitist political system that connived with the Church to keep ordinary people ignorant and powerless, and to deny them the most basic human rights.

This was the Mexico that existed from the early 1500s until the early 1900s when a revolution by the poor and downtrodden people swept away the power of the Church, and initiated a very slow process of reforming the government that is still going on today.

Most of the inhuman social policies of discrimination that were characteristic of Mexico for so many generations have been dramatically changed. But economic inequalities and endemic corruption are still embedded in the culture.

On a personal basis, however, the positive elements in the character of Mexicans generally outweigh the negative factors, making the average Mexican thoughtful, generous, kind, given to the pleasures of life, and incredibly proud of being Mexican.

This pride is something that most Americans are either not aware of, or ignore—and few Americans are fully familiar with the early history of Mexican-American relations. In addition to having invaded Mexico twice and having seized over half of the country's national territory, until relatively recent times Americans living along the U.S.-Mexico border typically treated Mexicans with arrogant disdain—if not outright contempt.

For most present-day Americans, Mexico is still an "undiscovered country," and it is not easy to know because, as Mexicans say, it is unique. It must be experienced over a period of time, without reservations or prejudices—and one must be intimately familiar with the history of the country—to fully understand and appreciate the richness of its unique culture; to truly know what it means to be Mexican, the good and the bad.

The following terms go a long way toward explaining why Mexicans think and behave the way they do—and why it is important for Americans and others to see beyond the negative image that has long been attached to the word "Mexican."

[1]
A Cultural Key to the Mexican Mindset

ONE OF THE most prominent elements in Mexican culture is subsumed in the word *simpatico* (seem-PAH-tee-coh)—a term that most English-speaking people who are somewhat familiar with the Spanish language assume means "being sympathetic," and let it go at that.

But in its Mexican context being *simpatico* means a lot more than just intellectual understanding and extending verbal sympathy. That definition, in fact, hardly touches on the real cultural nuances of the term.

In *Why Mexicans Think and Behave the Way They Do!* my explanation is that the term goes way beyond the English connotation of the word; that it infers that a *simpatico* person is also loyal, trustworthy and supportive, and can be counted on in times of trouble to do everything possible to help family and friends...and there is more.

A s*impatico* person is also one who understands your situation and agrees with your viewpoint—a concept that Americans and other English-speaking people do not necessarily relate to being sympathetic.

We often take the position that we are sympathetic about a problem, but in many cases our reaction is it's your problem, not ours, and you are on your own. That is not the Mexican way, and for this reason Mexicans feel that Americans are not as humane, not as generous, as we like to think we are.

To qualify for being described as *simpatico* in Mexican terms you have to be willing to go all the way in catering to and taking responsibility for the feelings and welfare of family members, close friends, co-workers and employees.

This cultural factor is just as important in business and political relationships as it is on a personal family level, and can make the difference between successful and unsuccessful relationships.

Facts, logic and other elements such as rapid progress and profits that are generally at the forefront of the Roman-Greek-Anglo way of thinking and doing things come second or third in the Mexican mindset.

The role and importance of the *simpatico* element in Mexican culture was an outgrowth of the extreme social, political and economic discrimination experienced by Indians and Spanish-Indian mixed-bloods from the latter part of the 1600s until well into the 20th century.

Writer Harriet Murray says that before the arrival of the Spaniards in 1620 some Mexican Indians believed that there was an organ near the heart that became known in Spanish as *El Grande Simpatico*, or "The Great Sympathetic Thing," that was the site of the soul, controlled the flow of the life force through the body, and became unbalanced when ignored or misused, eventually "dying" if such behavior continued.

This belief helped sustain the Indians who survived the arrival and aftermath of the Spanish, and as the population of mixed-bloods spiraled upward and their situation deteriorated they also began emphasizing goodwill and cooperation among their own kind as a defense against the ill-will and discriminatory policies imposed on them by those in power.

This defense mechanism gradually became subsumed in the single word *simpatico*, and took on a life of its own in the culture of the mixed-bloods—and as their numbers grew over the generations and they became more prominent in Mexican society the *simpatico* concept and practice gradually seeped upward into the ruling class as well.

The *simpatico* factor remains one of the most conspicuous and attractive elements in present-day Mexican culture. It is one of the first things that foreigners become aware of in their dealings with Mexicans—and is also one of the primary reasons why so many foreigners who spend any time in the country end up becoming permanent residents.

As writer Murray points out, in Mexico you don't have to feel guilty about not working all of the time, about not accomplishing anything of consequence every day, adding that this emotional and spiritual quality of life is also one of the things that draws Mexicans back to their homeland after they have spent time abroad—especially in the U.S., where this view of life is virtually non-existent.

Americans in particular who go to Mexico on business will find that the quality of their lives and their success in business will be greatly enhanced if they adopt the *simpatico* way of the country.

For a detailed review of the character and personality of Mexicans, see my book: *Why Mexicans Think and Behave the Way They Do!*

[2]
Mexican Truth vs. Real Truth

JUST AS THERE is Mexican time in the culture of Mexico and American time in American culture, there is also Mexican truth and real truth. And again, this element in

Mexican culture is a product of the convoluted history of the country.

From the beginning of the Spanish colonial period in Mexico in 1521 until the end of the Mexican Revolution in 1921 people who were not of pure Spanish ancestry and especially the native Indians, were subject to the will and the whims of medieval church dogma and doctrine, political leaders who were absolute dictators, a ruthless military, a corrupt police force and a cadre of local bosses who were typically despotic in their treatment of workers.

In this environment, the mixtures and Indians created their own version of *la verdad* (lah vahr-DAD), or the truth, making it whatever would help protect them from the arbitrary and often brutal dictates of the people who ruled the country for their own personal benefit...and for the first 300 years for the benefit of Spain.

For their own part, the ruling elite and their lackeys on whatever level were themselves under no legal or spiritual restraints to be truthful, even among themselves, and thus the whole culture operated under false pretenses, with reality obscured by masks of piety and gaiety.

When Mexican gained its freedom from Spain in 1821 after a long and bloody war, the country was ruled by a succession of dictators until 1921, following an even bloodier revolution that lasted for ten years.

In the 1920s, for the first time in the history of the country, laws were passed protecting some of the rights of common people. But still today ordinary Mexicans will tell you that the laws of the country that are supposed to protect them are like rubber—always subject to being stretched by those charged with enforcing them.

And some Mexicans still today will automatically respond with the partial truth or no truth at all even when there is no immediate threat to them on the basis that there could be some kind of threat in the future. But better education and more real personal freedom are slowly changing this built-in behavior.

For foreigners doing business with Mexicans the way to avoid having to deal with part-truth or no truth is to develop a solid relationship of respect and trust with the individuals concerned.

Mexicans have powerful historical reasons for disliking and distrusting the United States in particular and Americans in general. In 1845 Americans seized the Mexican province of Texas. Following the U.S.-Mexican war of 1846-1848 the U.S. annexed approximately half of the remaining territory of Mexico.

In the last decades of the 1800s and early decades of the 1900s American business barons, in cahoots with General Porfirio Diaz who ruled the country from 1876 to 1911, owned and or controlled over half of the economy of Mexico, and made little or no effort to end the economic and social bondage of the farming and laboring classes of Mexicans.

Nowadays, well over half of the wealth and economy of Mexico remains in the hands of about fifteen families.

Despite this sorry record, most ordinary Mexicans are naturally friendly, hospitable and generous toward Americans and other foreigners, and when they are met with honesty and goodwill they respond in kind. Most foreigners who spend any time in Mexico find the humanistic view and way of life so seductive and satisfying they fall in love with it.

Those who stay on and do well in Mexico are those who come to understand *la verdad* in the context of Mexican culture and become adept at living with and using it.

[3]
The Personalization Factor
In Mexican Behavior

ONE OF THE first things that foreigners in Mexico—
whether businesspeople or tourists—should know about
Mexicans is that their behavior, both private and official, is
generally controlled by their code of *personalismo* (pehr-
so-nah-LEES-moh), which results in them personalizing
everything.

Broadly speaking, *personalismo* embodies the Mexican
belief that personal dignity and self-interest take precedence over all other considerations, including the ethical
and moral. And as always in the character and personality
of Mexicans, this cultural trait originated during the three
hundred year reign of Spanish overlords.

During that long colonial period the principle of *personalismo* eventually came to override virtually everything else in the lives on non-Spanish Mexicans because
they were not fully protected by any cultural concept of
human rights or by any laws designed to guarantee such
rights.

When the Spanish period ended in 1821 it became common for presidents, officials, generals, business tycoons
and other people in positions of power to surround themselves with their kin, friends and close followers and to use
their power to enrich themselves and their followers.

Despite fundamental improvements in the legal and
justice systems in Mexico since the 1910-1921 Revolution
these self-serving practices remain deeply embedded in the

culture and continue to have a negative influence on the politics and the economy of the country.

Another thing that foreigners in Mexico must keep in mind and understand is that Mexican law is based on the Napoleonic Code, not English jurisprudence, which means in effect that people apprehended by the law for any reason, justified or not, are presumed guilty until proven innocent, and are generally treated as such.

Because of this system it became common for people who had been arrested to buy their way out of the clutches of the police, whether they were innocent or guilty. The overall situation in Mexico has improved considerably but according to reports arbitrary arrest, illegal detention—and torture—still occurs.

Fair play and justice have long been recognized in Mexico, but still today they remain arbitrary and subject to the interpretation of individual policemen, military officers and special security forces.

Foreign businesspeople in Mexico are advised to keep the *personalismo* factor in mind at all times and to make friends with people in high places not only to help guide them in the subtle intricacies of staying on good terms with people but also to come to their rescue if they have an encounter with any of the several law or security forces in Mexico that have or assume the privilege of arresting and holding people.

[4]
The Importance of Courtesy
in Mexico

THE HIGHER THE social level of Mexicans the more courteous they tend to be—but even the poorest Mexicans typically behave in an exceptionally courteous manner when in their normal environment, especially when compared to Americans.

The exceptional *cortesia* (cohr-tay-SEE-ah), or courtesy, of Mexicans had some of its roots in the rituals of the Catholic Church brought to Mexico from the 1500s on, but more so in the manners and customs of the early Spanish overlords who generally based their own etiquette on that of the Royal Court of Spain.

Another key element in the importance of courtesy in Mexican culture was its relationship with *dignidad* [deeg-nee-DAHD] or dignity, which had also become one of the most important elements in the character and personality of Mexicans during the Spanish regime..

Treated as virtual lepers from around 1600 until well into the 1900s, Mexico's racial mixtures, both men and women, created a virtual reality for themselves that was based on a high level of dignity and courtesy—two of the elements of Spanish culture they were free to emulate.

But long before the arrival of the conquistadors who conquered Mexico, the Aztecs and other Indians of Mexico had developed even more dignified and stylized societies than the Europeans, with sophisticated manners that were both prescribed and enforced.

These elements, again combined with the fact that for more than 400 years common Mexicans were forced to create a virtual reality for themselves, resulted in courtesy becoming a primary trait in the character of racially mixed Mexicans.

Modern-day younger Mexicans, fed a diet of American and Mexican pop culture, are losing some of the legacy of *cortesia*, but among the general population it is still significant enough that it remains a distinguishing characteristic of Mexicans and adds a special charm to life in the country.

Personal *dignidad* also remains one of the most important cultural factors in the lives of Mexicans, and men in particular often go to extraordinary lengths to protect their "face"—their image of themselves as men.

Young women who reject the advances of men must be extraordinarily careful not to trigger the male sense of being shamed—of having their manhood ignored or denied. Young men who slight the self-image of other men often put themselves in even more danger.

It is therefore important for foreigners visiting Mexico and dealing with Mexicans abroad to be aware of this special sensitivity and take pains not to insult the *dignidad* of Mexicans by behaving in what Mexicans consider an uncultured, rude manner.

This is not to say or imply that foreigners should act in an obsequious manner toward Mexican men [and women!] but it is very important to treat them with a higher level of courtesy than is characteristic of American behavior.

Such courtesy can and often does mean the difference between success and failure in Mexico. And the experience of many foreign old-timers in Mexico clearly demonstrates that it is just as important to be courteous to the lowest level of employees or individuals in general as it is to the socially and economically elite.

The Mexican saying, *Como Mexico no hay dos!* [coh-moh MEH-he-coh no aye dohss!], "There is no other country like Mexico!" is true—and should not be forgotten. One historical factor that helps explain the differences that one encounters in Mexico is that there is a strong Oriental theme in the culture—particularly among Indians and mixed-bloods.

[5]
Dealing with Mexico's Circumstantial Morality

AMERICANS WHO attempt to engage in business or make political deals with Mexicans are invariably confronted by a cultural barrier that must be overcome before they can succeed.

One of the fundamental truths of any society is that without a benign, humane, just, and efficient system of government the attitudes and behavior of the people in that country will be determined by their desire to survive rather than by religious beliefs or laws.

Mexico is a good example of a country that has been plagued by cultural weaknesses and failures resulting from anti-human policies and practices since it was forged in a cauldron of violence and bloodshed in the early 16th century—a heritage that continues to define and control the national character of the people in many ways.

The attempts to merge Moorish, Spanish and native Indian cultures is still incomplete, and continues to have a negative impact on the country. One of the primary cultural factors that evolved from this attempt is the ongoing role and importance of emotion in the lives of Mexicans.

This emotional factor has, in fact, been responsible for much of the inequalities and violence that have been endemic in Mexico since the arrival of the conquistadors in 1619. But it also gave birth to an aspect of Mexican culture that is aesthetically, spiritually and intellectually pleasing.

While the emotional factor is one of the most positive elements in Mexico's multi-faceted culture, is also the source of many of the negative elements that continue to plague the country, including the Mexican version of *moralidad* [mo-rah-lee-dahd] or morality.

In essence, Mexican morality is circumstantial. It is not and never has been a black-and-white proposition despite the powerful image and influence of the Catholic Church. It has, in fact, always been situational, depending on the circumstances of the time and place.

The reason for this is because from its inception in the early 1520s until recent times Mexico had no laws—religious or secular—that protected the rights of ordinary people. Both the Church and all levels of government were predatory, using the people, taking from them, and often abusing them in terrible ways.

Because the people had no system of security they could depend upon they had to react to each situation that arose on the basis of what would be least likely to bring harm to them, and most likely to help them. They were forced to become experts at creating morality on the spot.

The heritage of this long history of abuse has not fully disappeared from Mexico and continues to give business and social relations a unique Mexican color and tone. But, that is not to say there are no people in Mexico who behave in a truly moral manner. There are—especially in the poor classes and among women.

And as in virtually all societies, the women of Mexico are more rational and moral than the men because they must deal with the realities of life on a daily basis, while many of the men, especially the younger ones, tend to live in a virtual reality that they themselves create out of the legacy of their convoluted history.

Americans in particular tend to find Mexican *moralidad* a barrier until they have been immersed in the culture for several years and learn how to flow with it. And this learning process begins and ends with understanding and accepting the fact that Mexican behavior is very personal, very emotional, and these needs must be met before solid, productive relationships can be forged.

[6]

The Mexican Need for Respect!

OVER THE YEARS I have asked many Mexicans to tell me the most important word in the Mexican language. Most men have automatically said *respeto* (ray-SPAY-toh), or "respect," without having to think about it.

Much of this need for respect had its origins in the powerful *machismo (mah-CHEES-moh"* or "masculinity cult" element in Mexican culture, brought to Mexico by the Spanish conquistadors—who had adopted it from the Islamic Berber-Moors who dominated huge areas of Spain for some 800 years [711-1492].

But the primary factor in the Mexican need for respect had its origins in the Spanish policy of miscegenation with the native Indian women to produce a new race of mixed-bloods—the aim being to replace the native Indian population with people who would be more receptive to Spanish culture and therefore more valuable to Spain.

Spain's miscegenation policy began even before the small band of conquistadors had conquered Mexico. With the conquest of Mexico complete [1521], the conquerors and the new arrivals from Spain [administrators and soldiers] began impregnating as many Indian girls and women as possible on a massive scale—a phenomenon that was to create an astounding number of *Mestizos* [mixed-bloods] in the next one hundred years.

The first generation of mixed-bloods sired by the conquistadors were treated with respect and integrated into the mainstream of life in Mexico. But with the passing of the original conquerors mixed-bloods were gradually relegated to the lowest rungs of the social classes, just above Indians and dogs. The majority, who lived in Mexico City, became known as *leperos* (lay-paay-rohs) or "social lepers."

This disrespectful treatment of the growing Mestizo population created an intense hunger for respect in the mindset of mixed-blood males—and was passed on from one generation to the next, gradually becoming an integral part of their character.

In a desperate attempt to gain some self-respect urban mixed-blood men began to adopt the macho mentality and behavior of their Spanish overlords, and as the generations passed their demands for respect from other Mestizo men and women were routinely carried to the extreme.

By 1810, when Mexicans revolted against Spanish rule, the number of mixed-bloods had passed that of the pure Spanish members of the population, and continued to spiral upward. But it was to be another hundred years and a revolution against home-grown dictators and the smothering Catholic Church before they began to overcome the stigma of their race and participate in all areas of life in Mexico in large numbers.

Today, social class in Mexico is gradually becoming based more on education, occupation and financial status than on blood. But the heritage of over 400 years of discrimination and mistreatment has left its mark on the mindset of the typical Mexican.

While the combination of extreme arrogance and extreme humility that was characteristic of earlier generations of mixed-blood Mexicans has been dramatically muted, much of it is still present just below the surface and must be recognized and dealt with in an enlightened and humane manner in order to gain and keep their goodwill and cooperation.

Still today there are few things that are more likely to upset Mexicans in all classes than failure to show them respect. Being aware of the Mexican need for respect, and how to respond to it, is one of the first lessons that foreign businesspeople must learn if they want to succeed in Mexico.

This does not mean that foreigners need to flatter Mexicans in order to get along with them and work with them cooperatively. It simply means that they want and expect to be treated with conspicuous courtesy, honesty, fairness, and genuine goodwill.

[7]
The Importance of Dignity
in Mexico

AMERICANS AND OTHERS have long had distorted views of Mexico, including a romantic-roughish image that was portrayed by Hollywood and was in fact based on facts [carefully selected and massaged], along with an image of Mexican bandits and revolutionaries swathed in gun-belts that was also true in its time and place.

The cultural elements that were responsible for the creation of these images still exist in only slightly altered form, and without specific knowledge of the existence and role of these factors in present-day Mexican society foreigners interacting with Mexicans for business, political and personal reasons are at a disadvantage.

One of the most important of the cultural elements in the make-up of Mexicans—the romantic as well as the rogue aspects—is the importance of *dignidad* (deeg-nee-DAHD), or dignity, in Mexican life.

During the Spanish reign in Mexico [from 1521 to 1820] the Indians and rapidly growing number of Mestizos (Spanish-Indian mixed-bloods) had few if any rights of full citizenship and few choices in how they behaved.

One choice they gradually assumed by osmosis, however, was copying some of the behavior of their Spanish overlords, particularly their exaggerated sense of self-image. Mestizo men in particular began compensating for their slave-like social and political status and their abject poverty by developed an extreme sense of pride and dignity.

For many generations this sense of exaggerated pride and dignity resulted in Mexico being one of the most violent societies on the planet. Most men carried guns and used them at the slightest hint of an insult or aggression. It was not until well into the 20th century that the majority of Mexican men stopped carrying weapons at all times.

Personal *dignidad* is still one of the most important cultural factors in the lives of Mexicans, and men in particular often go to extraordinary lengths to protect their "face"—their image of themselves as masculine men.

It is therefore important for foreigners visiting Mexico and dealing with Mexicans abroad to be aware of this special sensitivity and take pains not to insult their typically strong sense of *dignidad*.

Middle-class Anglo-Americans, who are generally the least dignified and mannered people on the scene, especially when they are abroad, should make a point of being less boisterous and less informal, and more reserved in their speech and behavior when in Mexico.

One of the things that Mexicans, Asians and many Europeans find so disconcerting about Americans is that our behavior is so unstructured they cannot predict what we are going to say or do…and that creates a sense of ill-ease.

Mexicans love a good time and they can be as unrestrained in their behavior as anyone, but in Mexico there is a time and place for such behavior, and the separation of decorum and rambunctiousness is generally strict.

Businesspeople and others dealing with Mexicans in Mexico and abroad will find their relationships much more positive if they exercise a noticeable degree of decorum in their own behavior.

It is important to keep in mind that in broad terms, the foundation of Mexican behavior in all of their relationships —business, political and social—is emotional and per-

sonal...a circumstance that is often diametrically opposed
to the American way of thinking and doing things.

[8]
Fixing and Maintaining
Responsibility in Mexico

ONE OF THE cultural factors that must be taken into
consideration when doing business in Mexico is the built-
in tendency of most Mexicans to avoid taking personal
responsibility for their behavior in personal affairs, in their
work, or in other matters. And the reason for this is, of
course, historical.

For most of the 300-year reign of Spain in Mexico
[1521-1821] the Spanish overlords treated the native Indian populations as if they were incapable of sophisticated
reasoning and unable to take responsibility for their behavior.

Their treatment of the growing number of Indian-
Spanish mixed-bloods [Mestizos] was to eventually follow
the same pattern. The number of mix-bloods in Mexico
ballooned exponentially after the Spanish conquered the
country because it was policy of the conquerors and later
Spanish administrators and soldiers to impregnate as many
Indian women as possible.

In the beginning the rational for this program of miscegenation was to create as many non-Indian people as
possible because Indians were not liked or trusted, and it
was presumed that a growing population of mixed-bloods
would benefit both Mexico and Spain.

However, with the passing of the conquistadors who had conquered Mexico, and who had taken the lead in implementing the miscegenation policy, the social status of the Indian-Spanish mixtures rapidly degenerated to the point that they became even more disliked and distrusted than the Indians.

As time passed, this generations-long policy of denying Indians and racial mixtures the opportunity to get positions of responsibility [other than hereditary positions among the Indian tribes] left the bulk of Mexico's population with no experienced in handling responsibility and little if any incentive to do so.

It became natural for workmen to wait for precise orders from their bosses before doing anything—and often when something went wrong they would remain silent, waiting for the boss to discover the problem and give them new orders. The concept of personal *responsibilidad* (ray-spon-sah-bee-lee-dahd) was simply not a part of their mindset.

Freedom from Spain in 1821 did not significantly change the culture that the Spaniards had forged. Most Mestizos and Indians were to remain poverty-stricken and powerless for 100-plus more years, and subject to a degree of official discrimination that prevented them from getting into positions of responsibility.

The exceptions to this were the Mestizos who left the urban areas of central Mexico in the early 1800s for the mostly unoccupied northern territories where they were free to take the initiative in improving their lives. Some of them became successful ranchers and businesspeople. Others became bandits.

Still today managers in Mexico must deal with the reluctance of many workers to take personal responsibility for their actions, even though this cultural factor is changing with better education and the spread of American influence in the country.

As with arriving at *la verdad,* or the truth, in Mexico, creating an environment in which individual Mexicans take responsibility for their actions it is a matter of developing personal relationships based on trust and respect.

For employers this means taking a personal interest in the employees themselves as well as in their families, including any health problems or other factors that affect them. Visiting a family member in a hospital, for example, can get you a lot of loyalty and cooperation from employees.

[9]
How Culture
Circumvents the Law in Mexico

WHEN THE SPANISH *conquistadors* [conquerors] conquered Mexico in 1521 the "laws" they themselves followed and began attempting to impose on the large native Indian population were a mishmash of Catholic dogma and Islamic customs.

Following the successful Mexican rebellion against Spain three hundred years later [1810-1821] the new Mexican government instituted a variety of reforms in the legal system that were to be on the books until the early 1860s, but generally were not enforced.

In 1862 French forces, along with British and Spanish contingents, invaded and captured Mexico, ostensibly because the government of the newly elected president, Benito Juarez [a Zatopec Indian], refused to continue paying onerous debts to these countries.

With the French in power in Mexico, Napoleon III appointed Maximilian [a member of royal family of Hapsburg] as the emperor of Mexico. His regime made the Napoleonic Code [promulgated by the original Napoleon in 1804] the law of the land.

However, Maximilian himself didn't last long. Mexican nationalists [with help from the U.S.] defeated the French forces and their allies in 1867, the Mexican government was restored, and Emperor Maximilian was executed by a firing squad.

But the Napoleonic Code remained the foundation of the legal system, and despite a series of reforms following the Mexican revolution against home-grown dictatorships [1910-1921] and other reforms during the rest of the century, the ancient French Code remains the basic foundation of Mexico's legal system today.

However, culture generally continues to play a greater role in present-day Mexico than the legal system, and this means that many of the attitudes and customs that developed in Mexico during the Spanish era as well as that of the following dictatorships take precedence over laws.

Fair play and justice have, of course, long been recognized in Mexico, but still today they remain arbitrary and subject to the interpretation of individual policemen, military officers and special security forces. Self-serving practices that ignore the law remain deeply embedded in the culture and continue to have a negative influence on the politics and the economy of the country.

Foreigners in Mexico should keep in mind that under Mexican law people apprehended by law enforcement agents for any reason, justified or not, are presumed guilty until proven innocent, and are generally treated as such.

Because of this system it became common long ago for people who had been arrested to buy their way out of the clutches of the police if they could afford it, whether they were innocent or guilty. The overall situation in Mexico has improved considerably but arbitrary arrest, illegal detention—and torture—still occurs.

Foreign businesspeople in Mexico are advised to keep these factors in mind at all times and to make friends with people who can help guide them in the subtle intricacies of staying on good terms with everyone as well as to come to their rescue If they have an encounter with any of the several law or security forces in Mexico that have or assume the privilege of arresting and holding people.

[10]
Machismo
(Mah-CHEES-moh)
The Cult of Masculinity

MEXICAN WRITERS like the great Octavio Paz say that Mexico's famous (or infamous) *machismo* (mah-CHEES-moh) cult of male masculinity was a direct result of the Spanish overlords exercising their power to have sexual relations with any Indian or Mestizo female that caught their eye.

Prevented from taking any action when they saw their daughters, girl friends and wives being sexually used by the overlords, the Mestizos in particular created a new world of hyper sexuality for themselves, taking their normal sexuality to the extremes and becoming more aggressive toward women and more demanding in their relationships.

This attitude typically resulted in men becoming intensely angry when any women rejected their advances and often mounting elaborate campaigns to have the women one way or the other. Another side of this fierce sexuality was that once the men had the women they had targeted their ardor often vanished and they walked away, resulting in huge numbers of children being born to young unmarried girls.

Most Mexican men are still caught up in their macho image of themselves, but it is now generally much less hyper than it was for so many generations, and the higher one goes up the social ladder the more it is cloaked in sophisticated etiquette and often elaborate courting rituals.

As in the past the machoism of Mexican men does not always lead to marriage, so there is still a disproportionate number of children born out of wedlock.

Americans in Mexico should handle the macho topic with care and diplomacy—especially since the same hyper sense of sexuality exists among some minorities in the U.S.

[11]
Chistes
(Chees-tehs)
The Role of Sardonic Jokes in Mexico

MEXICAN MEN, particularly those in the poor classes, have traditionally had a sardonic sense of humor that evolved from the helplessness of their social, economic and political situation under the smothering Church, the rapacious government, and the brutality of the law enforcement agencies.

This humor, in the form of *chistes* (chees-tehs) or jokes, was used to help the men put up with their situation and was invariable aimed at institutions and leaders that controlled their lives and made it difficult or impossible for them to realize their ambitions for a better life.

The Catholic Church was one of the institutions that was most often slammed by this humor because it exercised such pervasive control over the poor and disenfranchised— especially the women who generally speaking were the only ones deeply influenced by the precepts of the Church.

The next most popular subject for sardonic humor in recent times has been politicians and bureaucrats who are primarily out to enrich themselves and their families. As in the United States, lawyers in Mexico are also a favorite target of biting humor.

Much of the male humor in Mexico, among the poor as well as the middle and upper classes, is (not surprisingly) sexual in nature. It is also often self-deprecating, which takes some of the sting out.

Here again, is another cultural area where foreign residents and visitors should tred lightly. Mexicans generally accept such forms of humor from other Mexicans, but not from foreigners.

[12]
Some Reminders About Mexican Etiquette & Business Customs

PERSONAL ETIQUETTE in Mexico tends to be more formal and more important, on every level of society, than in the United States—a factor that can upset Mexicans who are not familiar with the free-wheeling ways of most Americans, or regard it as a cultural failing if not an indication of disrespect for Mexican culture.

The higher one goes on the social ladder in Mexico the more formal and the more institutionalized the behavior one encounters. Some business and personal customs in Mexico are also different from those that are common in the U.S.

In purely social settings, adult women who are friends usually greet each other with a kiss each on the cheek—or make the motion of kissing. The formal greeting for male friends is an *abrazo* [hug] combined with two or three pats on the back. In business settings both men and women shake hands.

Business meetings combined with breakfast and lunch are as common in Mexico as they are in the U.S. and many other countries. At these meetings, business matters are generally not discussed until near the end of the meal. Earlier conversations are generally devoted to talking about personal matters, particularly family affairs and sports. For newcomers to Mexico this is a time for getting acquainted and bonding.

It is customary for foreigners going to Mexico on business to take small gifts for the people they are scheduled to meet— particularly those who come to the airport to pick them up but for others as well. You can get special mileage by taking gifts for the children of contacts you are to meet. Business gifts are also a part of the protocol in Mexico, and during the Christmas season they can be lavish.

Tipping baggage carriers, taxi drivers, bellhops, waiters and others in personal service industries has long been common in Mexico because salaries in these areas have traditionally been low by any standard. For service in places that present bills, tips usually range from 10 to 20 percent of the bills. When there is no bill, such as in the case of baggage handlers, bellhops, barbers, parking lot attendants and gas station attendants, the amount of the tip is arbitrary...and depends more on the affluence and generosity of the tipper.

In dining and drinking situations when there are two or three people, or sometimes more, it is common for the senior person to pay the bill. Or if a group meets often, and the members of the group are in or close to the same age and income level, they often take turns paying.

As a rule, it is customary for Mexicans to treat foreign visitors as their guests and to insist on paying dining and drinking bills—making sure they get their hands on the bills first; or they leave the table before the party ends and pay the bill discreetly. In such cases, the foreign visitor should make sure he or she returns the hospitality at the next opportunity.

Mexicans have traditionally been more clothes-conscious than Americans because one's dress was closely associated with social class. The social implications of dress are less direct now, but most adult Mexicans are still more formal in both their casual and business attire than typical Americans.

Wearing shorts and sandals, for example, is generally a dead giveaway that one is a foreigner. In classier restaurants and clubs casual clothing is usually taboo.

Mexicans are especially sensitive about rank and professional titles, and the custom of using appropriate titles should be followed by foreign businesspeople until they have established good personal relations with their individual contacts. It is therefore important for newcomers to Mexico to inquire about the titles of the people they are scheduled or want to meet.

In social situations Mexicans are more laid back in their view and use of time. It is a deeply established custom to arrive at such meetings anywhere from half an hour to an hour later than the pre-set time.

Visitors to Mexico for whatever purpose who go shopping should keep in mind that bargaining is customary in open-air markets. The custom is to start out offering half of the listed price, and go up from there.

✳✳✳

www.ingramcontent.com/pod-product-compliance
Lightning Source LLC
Chambersburg PA
CBHW020208200326
41521CB00005BA/287